Pro-Course For Integrated Marketing Communications

Harmonizing Your Message Across Advertising, PR, and Digital Channels

Aziza Tawfiq Abdelghafar

DEDICATION

For those who dare to dream, persist through challenges, and embrace the journey of lifelong learning. Your resilience shapes the future.

Table of contents

Module 1: Fundamentals and Strategic Overview — 15

Lesson 1: Introduction to IMC	18
Lesson 2: IMC Components	24
Lesson 3: Building a Successful IMC Strategy	61
Practical Exercise	68
	71

Module 2: Aligning Messages Across Channels

Lesson 1: Consistency in Advertising Messages	74
Lesson 2: PR as Part of the IMC Strategy	81
Lesson 3: The Role of Digital Channels in Integration	87
Short Assignment	92
	95

Module 3: Effectively Managing Integrated Campaigns

Lesson 1: Setting KPIs	99
Lesson 2: Scheduling and Budget Allocation	104
Lesson 3: Managing Teams and Agencies	110
Hands-On Exercise	116

Module 4: Performance Measurement and Continuous Improvement

120

Lesson 1: Analytics and Tracking Tools	124
Lesson 2: Smart Reporting	130
Lesson 3: Optimization and Strategy Adjustment	134
Evaluation Task	138
	141

Capstone Project

ACKNOWLEDGMENTS

I am deeply grateful to everyone who played a role in bringing this book to life. To my family, whose unwavering support fuels my ambition; to my friends, who inspire and challenge me; and to my mentors and colleagues, whose insights and wisdom have guided my path. Your encouragement has been invaluable.

Thank you for believing in this journey.

About the Book

In today's fast-paced digital world, delivering a cohesive brand message across multiple channels is no longer optional — it's essential. *Pro-Course for Integrated Marketing Communications: Harmonizing Your Message Across Advertising, PR, and Digital Channels* is your ultimate guide to mastering the art and science of IMC.

This professional course breaks down the complexities of integrated marketing into actionable steps, helping you craft consistent, compelling messages that resonate with your audience — whether through advertising, public relations, or digital platforms. Packed with real-world insights, hands-on exercises, and strategic frameworks, this book equips marketers, business owners, and communication professionals with the tools they need to build, execute, and optimize high-impact campaigns.

Part of the *Pro-Course for Marketing* series, this book is designed for learners who want practical, results-driven knowledge — not just theory. By the end, you'll be able to align your brand's voice across all touchpoints, measure performance effectively, and adapt strategies for maximum engagement.

Preface

Marketing has evolved. Gone are the days when businesses could rely on a single channel—a TV ad, a billboard, or a newspaper feature—to reach their audience. Today, consumers interact with brands across multiple platforms, from social media and email to PR events and traditional ads. If your messages aren't unified, your brand risks sounding inconsistent, confusing, or worse—untrustworthy.

That's where **Integrated Marketing Communications (IMC)** comes in. IMC isn't just a buzzword; it's a strategic approach that ensures every piece of communication—whether an Instagram post, a press release, or a promotional offer—works together to tell one powerful story.

This book is designed to be your roadmap. Whether you're a marketing professional looking to sharpen your skills, a business owner managing your own campaigns, or a student eager to learn modern marketing strategies, this course will guide you through:

- **The fundamentals of IMC** – What it is, why it matters, and how it differs from traditional marketing.

- **Channel alignment** – How to craft a consistent message that adapts seamlessly to ads, PR, and digital platforms.

- **Campaign execution** – From setting KPIs to managing budgets and teams.

- **Measuring success** – Using analytics to refine strategies and boost ROI.

Each module includes practical exercises, real-world examples, and actionable takeaways so you can apply what you learn immediately. By the final capstone project, you'll have the confidence to design and launch a fully integrated campaign from scratch.

Marketing is about connection. And in a noisy, multi-channel world, integration isn't just helpful — it's the key to standing out. Let's get started.

—

The Pro-Course for Marketing Series

Course Introduction

What is Integrated Marketing Communications (IMC)?

Integrated Marketing Communications is more than just a strategy—it's the backbone of modern marketing. At its core, IMC is about unifying every message your brand puts out into the world, ensuring that whether someone sees an ad, reads a press release, or scrolls past a social media post, they experience the same clear and compelling story. Think of it as the harmony in an orchestra—each instrument (or marketing channel) plays its part, but together, they create something far more powerful than any single note.

The concept isn't entirely new, but its importance has skyrocketed in the digital age. Traditional marketing often treated channels like TV, print, and PR as separate entities, with different teams and disconnected goals. IMC flips that approach. Instead of silos, it builds bridges. It connects advertising, public relations, direct marketing, promotions, and digital platforms into a seamless system where each element reinforces the others. The result? A brand that feels consistent, trustworthy, and impossible to ignore.

But IMC isn't just about aesthetics—it's about impact. When messages align, they cut through the noise of today's crowded marketplace. Customers no longer interact with brands in a linear way. They might discover a product on Instagram, read a news article about the company, and then see a targeted ad—all in the same afternoon. If those touchpoints clash or contradict, confusion sets in. IMC eliminates that risk by making sure every piece of communication, no matter where it appears, reflects the same values, voice, and purpose.

Why is it essential in the digital age?

The digital revolution didn't just change how we market—it changed how audiences think. Consumers today are savvier, more skeptical, and bombarded with more content than ever before. They don't separate "online" and "offline" experiences; to them, it's all just part of how they engage with the world. A brand's Twitter feed is as much a representation of its identity as its customer service or its billboard ads. Fragmented messaging doesn't just look unprofessional—it erodes trust.

Consider this: a company launches a heartfelt ad campaign about sustainability, but its social media team accidentally shares a tone-deaf post about fast fashion the same week. Or a PR crisis erupts, but the marketing department keeps running upbeat ads as if nothing happened. These disconnects don't go unnoticed. Audiences spot inconsistencies instantly, and in an era where reputation spreads at the speed of a viral tweet, the cost of misalignment can be devastating.

IMC solves this by treating all communication as part of a single ecosystem. It ensures that a brand's environmental stance in its PR efforts matches its product packaging, its LinkedIn thought leadership, and its influencer partnerships. It's not about repeating the same words everywhere—it's about adapting a core message to fit each channel while keeping the essence intact. A tweet might be witty, a press release formal, and an ad emotional, but they all point back to the same truth about who the brand is and why it matters.

Beyond trust, IMC drives efficiency. When teams collaborate instead of working in isolation, budgets stretch further. A social media campaign can amplify a PR event. An email series can reinforce an ad's call-to-action. Data from digital ads can inform which PR narratives resonate most. Without integration, marketers waste resources reinventing the wheel for each channel. With it, every dollar and every effort compounds.

What will you learn in this course?

This book isn't a theoretical lecture—it's a hands-on guide to building and executing campaigns that work. You'll start by mastering the foundations: what IMC really means (and what myths to avoid), how it differs from old-school marketing, and why some brands fail at integration while others thrive. Then, you'll dive into the practical tools. You'll learn how to dissect a target audience so thoroughly that you can predict which channels will reach them best. You'll practice crafting a "message architecture"—a flexible yet unshakable core idea that can adapt to a TikTok video or a shareholder report without losing its soul.

The middle modules tackle execution. You'll explore how to structure ads that feel cohesive with PR narratives, how to weave digital and traditional media into a single strategy, and how to avoid the "Frankenstein campaign" trap (where disjointed tactics create a monster instead of a masterpiece). There's a focus on teamwork, too—because IMC isn't a solo act. You'll get frameworks for aligning departments, briefing agencies, and managing the inevitable hiccups that come with complex campaigns.

Later sections focus on measurement and agility. You'll learn to track what actually matters (not just vanity metrics), interpret data without drowning in spreadsheets, and tweak campaigns in real time. Case studies reveal how brands like Dove, Nike, and startups you've never heard of used IMC to punch above their weight. By the capstone project, you'll design a full campaign from scratch, blending advertising, PR, and digital—with ready-to-use templates to jumpstart real work.

Who is this book for?

If you're holding this book, you're likely someone who understands that marketing today can't be piecemeal. Maybe you're a mid-career marketer tired of channel-specific KPIs and want to think bigger. Maybe you're a small business owner wearing ten hats, needing a system to make your limited resources feel cohesive. Or perhaps you're a student or career-switcher who senses that the future of marketing is integration, but aren't sure where to start.

This course speaks to doers, not just theorists. It's for the PR professional who wants to prove how their work fuels sales, the social media manager tired of posts that feel disconnected from the brand's ads, the entrepreneur who knows their messaging is uneven but lacks the blueprint to fix it. No jargon-filled fluff— just actionable steps, relatable examples, and the confidence to unify your voice across every platform that matters.

The digital age doesn't reward fragmentation. Whether you're promoting a product, a nonprofit, or your personal brand, IMC is the difference between being heard and being forgotten. This book is your roadmap to making sure your message isn't just seen—but remembered.

Module 1: Fundamentals and Strategic Overview

Lesson 1: Introduction to IMC

Lesson 2: IMC Components

Lesson 3: Building a Successful IMC Strategy

Practical Exercise

Module 1: Fundamentals and Strategic Overview

Before you can run, you need to understand the ground beneath your feet. This first module is where we lay the foundation for everything that follows in your Integrated Marketing Communications journey. Think of it as learning the rules of the road before you start driving — except here, the road is the complex, ever-changing landscape of modern marketing, and the vehicle is your ability to craft messages that move people.

This isn't about abstract theories or fluffy concepts. It's about the real building blocks of IMC — the core principles that separate scattered, inconsistent messaging from campaigns that feel cohesive, intentional, and impossible to ignore. We'll start by demystifying what IMC actually means (and what it doesn't), how it's fundamentally different from old-school marketing approaches, and why trying to "bolt on" integration after the fact never works.

Then, we'll break down the key components that make up IMC — advertising, PR, direct marketing, promotions, and digital channels — not as isolated tactics, but as interconnected tools in your toolkit. You'll see how each one plays a distinct role, and more importantly, how they amplify each other when used strategically.

Finally, we'll get practical. You'll learn how to build an IMC strategy from the ground up, starting with the most critical (and often overlooked) step: truly understanding your audience. Because without that, even the shiniest campaign will fall flat. You'll discover how to define a core message flexible enough to work across channels yet specific enough to be memorable, and how to choose the right mix of platforms to reach people where they actually pay attention.

By the end of this module, you won't just "get" IMC — you'll start seeing all the missed opportunities in the marketing around you. The billboards that clash with the brand's Twitter tone, the PR crises that could've been avoided with aligned messaging, the small businesses punching above their weight because they "get" integration. And with the hands-on exercise, you'll apply this lens to a real business, identifying exactly which IMC components would make the biggest impact.

This is where the magic starts — when you shift from seeing marketing as a series of disconnected tasks to a symphony of synchronized messages. Let's begin.

Lesson 1: Introduction to IMC

Imagine walking into a store where the salesperson greets you with enthusiasm, the packaging on the shelves tells a compelling story, and the follow-up email you receive later feels like a natural continuation of the conversation. Everything fits together seamlessly, creating an experience that feels intentional and memorable. Now imagine the opposite – a disjointed mess where the ads promise one thing, the website says another, and customer service seems unaware of both. The difference between these two scenarios comes down to one critical concept: Integrated Marketing Communications.

At its heart, IMC is about creating harmony across every touchpoint where your brand interacts with the world. It's the art and science of ensuring that whether someone encounters your brand through an advertisement, a news article, a social media post, or a promotional offer, they receive a consistent message that builds recognition and trust. This goes far beyond simply using the same logo colors everywhere. True integration means your brand's core identity – its values, personality, and promises – shines through clearly, no matter how or where someone experiences it.

The core principles of IMC revolve around unity, consistency, and strategic alignment. Unity means all your communication efforts work together toward common objectives rather than operating as separate islands. Consistency ensures your brand voice and messaging remain coherent across platforms and over time. Strategic alignment guarantees that every marketing activity ties back to your overall business goals, creating a cumulative effect where the whole becomes greater than the sum of its parts. These principles might sound simple, but implementing them requires careful planning, cross-departmental collaboration, and a deep understanding of how different communication channels work together.

One of the most powerful aspects of IMC is how it reflects how people actually experience brands today. Consumers don't categorize their interactions as "advertising" versus "PR" versus "social media" – to them, it's all just "Brand X." They might see a tweet in the morning, notice a billboard during their commute, read a blog mention at lunch, and get a promotional email in the evening. If these touchpoints contradict each other or feel disconnected, the brand appears disorganized or, worse, inauthentic. IMC eliminates this problem by designing all communications as parts of an interconnected system where each element reinforces the others.

Traditional vs. Integrated Communication

The shift from traditional marketing approaches to integrated communications represents one of the most significant evolutions in how businesses connect with their audiences. Traditional marketing often operated in silos, with separate teams handling advertising, public relations, sales promotions, and other functions with little coordination between them. The advertising team might develop a campaign without consulting the PR department, while the social media team pursued entirely different objectives. This fragmented approach made sense in an era when consumers experienced brands through limited, clearly separated channels – perhaps seeing TV ads at home, print ads in magazines, and encountering PR through newspaper articles.

But the media landscape has transformed dramatically. The lines between different types of communication have blurred, and consumers flow effortlessly between channels throughout their day. A customer might discover a product through an influencer's Instagram story, research it via Google searches that lead to news articles and blog posts, check the brand's own social media for social proof, then finally make a purchase after receiving a targeted email offer. In this environment, traditional siloed marketing doesn't just become inefficient – it actively works against creating a strong brand impression.

Integrated communication flips this model entirely. Instead of separate strategies for different channels, IMC starts with a unified strategic vision that then adapts to various platforms while maintaining core consistency. The advertising doesn't just coexist with PR efforts – they complement and amplify each other. The social media strategy doesn't run parallel to email campaigns – they're designed as different expressions of the same central narrative. This approach mirrors how people actually process brand information today, creating a more natural and persuasive brand experience.

Another crucial difference lies in measurement and accountability. Traditional marketing often judged success by channel-specific metrics – ad recall for television commercials, circulation numbers for print ads, opens and clicks for email campaigns. While these metrics remain important, IMC adds a layer of strategic evaluation that looks at how all these elements work together to drive meaningful business outcomes. Instead of just asking "Did people see our ad?" IMC asks "How did all our communications work together to move people through the customer journey?" This holistic perspective leads to smarter resource allocation and more impactful marketing overall.

The transition from traditional to integrated communication requires more than just organizational changes – it demands a shift in mindset. It means breaking down long-standing departmental barriers and fostering collaboration between specialists who may have previously worked in isolation. It requires developing messaging flexible enough to work across diverse platforms while remaining true to core brand identity. Most challengingly, it means resisting the temptation to judge individual components in isolation and instead evaluating how every piece contributes to the larger picture.

This integrated approach has become particularly crucial in the digital age, where consumers have more control over their brand interactions than ever before. People curate their own media diets, skipping ads they find irrelevant and seeking out content that resonates with them. In this environment, consistency and authenticity become paramount – consumers can spot inauthentic or disjointed messaging instantly, and they reward brands that deliver coherent, value-driven experiences across every touchpoint. IMC provides the framework to meet these heightened expectations while cutting through the noise of an oversaturated media landscape.

The contrast between traditional and integrated communication becomes especially apparent when looking at campaign examples. Consider a traditional product launch where the advertising team creates TV spots, the PR department secures magazine features, the digital team runs social media ads, and the sales team prepares in-store promotions – all developed separately with minimal coordination. Compare this to an integrated launch where all these elements share common visual language, messaging themes, and strategic objectives, each tailored to its specific medium while unmistakably part of a unified whole. The difference in impact and memorability is often dramatic.

Understanding this distinction between traditional and integrated approaches sets the foundation for everything that follows in developing effective IMC strategies. It's not about abandoning proven marketing principles but rather about evolving them for a world where consumers experience brands as seamless wholes rather than collections of separate communications. This perspective informs how we select channels, craft messages, allocate resources, and measure success – all topics we'll explore in depth throughout this course.

As we move forward, keep in mind that mastering IMC isn't about rigid formulas or one-size-fits-all solutions. The most effective integrated communications feel organic to the brand and authentic to the audience. They balance consistency with adaptability, maintaining core identity while flexing to different contexts. They measure success not just by impressions or engagement rates but by how effectively they build lasting relationships between brands and the people they serve. This is the art and science we'll be exploring together – not as abstract theory, but as practical knowledge you can apply immediately to create more powerful, cohesive marketing communications.

Lesson 2: IMC Components

Picture a master chef's kitchen. Just as a great meal comes from combining the right ingredients in perfect harmony, powerful marketing communications blend different components to create something greater than the sum of its parts. In this lesson, we'll explore the five essential ingredients of IMC - advertising, public relations, direct marketing, promotions, and digital channels - not as isolated elements, but as interconnected tools that work best when used together strategically.

Advertising forms the most visible layer of IMC, acting like the bold flavors in our kitchen metaphor. These are the paid messages designed to capture attention and shape perceptions, from television commercials to social media ads. But modern advertising in an IMC context isn't about shouting the loudest - it's about creating memorable, on-brand messages that start conversations rather than just broadcasting announcements. The best advertising today feels less like an interruption and more like valuable content, whether that's an entertaining video, a thought-provoking image, or useful information. When integrated properly, advertising doesn't stand alone but works in concert with other components - driving people to PR coverage, supporting promotional offers, or directing traffic to digital properties. The key is ensuring every ad, no matter the platform, reinforces the same core message while adapting to the unique strengths of each medium.

Public relations serves as the subtle seasoning that enhances all other flavors. Unlike advertising's paid approach, PR earns attention through media coverage, influencer partnerships, and community engagement. In an IMC strategy, PR isn't just about getting press mentions - it's about building credibility and shaping the narrative around your brand. A great PR effort might secure a feature article that validates your advertising claims, or arrange speaking opportunities that establish executives as thought leaders. The most integrated PR anticipates how media coverage will interact with other components - ensuring a product launch announcement aligns with advertising timing, or that crisis communications support (rather than contradict) marketing messages. PR also provides valuable third-party validation that makes advertising more believable and promotions more appealing.

Direct marketing acts as the precision cooking tools that deliver personalized experiences. Where advertising casts a wide net, direct marketing - whether through email, targeted mailers, or one-to-one messaging - speaks directly to individuals based on their specific needs and behaviors. In an integrated approach, direct marketing doesn't feel like spam but like a natural continuation of other brand interactions. Imagine someone sees your ad, then receives a perfectly timed email offering more information, followed by a special promotion tailored to their interests - that's direct marketing working in harmony with other components. The data gathered through direct interactions then feeds back into the system, helping refine advertising targeting, PR messaging, and promotional strategies.

Promotions provide the immediate incentives that drive action, like the finishing touches that make a dish irresistible. These limited-time offers, contests, and special deals gain much more power when integrated with other components. A promotion advertised through PR coverage, amplified by digital channels, and supported by direct marketing touches creates multiple touchpoints that reinforce each other. The key is ensuring promotions don't undermine but enhance brand perception - a luxury brand might focus on exclusive access rather than price discounts, while a value brand might emphasize savings. Well-integrated promotions feel like natural extensions of the brand story rather than disconnected gimmicks.

Digital channels serve as both the kitchen and the dining room in our metaphor - the space where all other components come together and where customers experience the final result. Websites, social media, search marketing, and other digital platforms don't exist separately in IMC but provide the connective tissue linking all efforts. A TV ad drives to a website that captures data for direct marketing. PR coverage includes social sharing options that spread the word digitally. Promotions get amplified through digital ads and email. What makes digital channels truly powerful in integration is their ability to provide real-time feedback, allowing marketers to see what's working and adjust other components accordingly.

The magic happens when these components stop competing and start collaborating. Consider how a product launch might flow across all five: PR builds anticipation with media previews, advertising creates broad awareness, direct marketing targets likely buyers, promotions provide incentive to purchase, and digital channels facilitate the actual transaction while collecting valuable data. Each component plays its role at the right time, with consistent messaging adapted to each format. The customer experiences this not as separate marketing efforts but as a cohesive journey with the brand.

Understanding these components as parts of an interconnected system changes how we approach each one. Advertising creative considers how it will be amplified through PR and digital sharing. PR strategies incorporate advertising schedules and promotional calendars. Direct marketing campaigns reference current advertising themes. Promotions get designed with digital fulfillment in mind. This holistic perspective prevents the common pitfalls of disjointed messaging, wasted resources, and missed opportunities that plague siloed marketing approaches.

The most effective IMC strategies don't give equal weight to all components but carefully select and balance them based on objectives, audience, and budget. A B2B technology company might emphasize PR and direct marketing with less focus on broad advertising. A consumer packaged goods brand might lead with advertising and promotions supported by digital engagement. The art lies in knowing which components to emphasize when, and how to make them all work together toward common goals.

As we move forward, keep in mind that these components are tools, not rules. The best integrated marketers understand the unique value each brings to the mix while remaining flexible enough to adapt their approach based on what the situation demands. In our increasingly complex media environment, this ability to blend traditional and digital, paid and earned, broad and targeted approaches separates effective communications from mere noise. The following sections will dive deeper into each component, but always with this integrative mindset - because in the kitchen of modern marketing, the most memorable experiences come from perfect combinations, not single ingredients.

Advertising in Integrated Marketing Communications

Advertising has always been the most visible and recognizable element of marketing communications—the billboards we pass on the highway, the commercials that interrupt our favorite shows, the sponsored posts that appear in our social media feeds. But in an integrated marketing strategy, advertising isn't just about grabbing attention—it's about starting meaningful conversations, reinforcing brand identity, and working in harmony with every other communication channel to create a seamless experience for the audience.

The role of advertising in IMC goes far beyond simply broadcasting a message. It serves as the anchor point that sets the tone for all other communications. When done right, advertising establishes the core narrative — the big idea that PR will amplify, promotions will incentivize, and digital channels will extend into interactive experiences. Think of it as the foundation of a house: if it's strong and well-built, everything else can stand firmly on top of it. But if it's shaky or inconsistent, the entire structure becomes unstable.

One of the biggest shifts in modern advertising within an IMC framework is the move from interruption to engagement. Traditional advertising often relied on disrupting what people were doing — stopping them during a TV show, standing out on a crowded magazine page, or popping up unexpectedly online. Today, the most effective ads don't feel like intrusions but like valuable content that fits naturally into the consumer's world. They entertain, inform, or solve problems while subtly reinforcing brand messaging. This approach makes advertising more welcome and more likely to be shared, discussed, and remembered — key factors in an integrated strategy where multiple touchpoints reinforce each other.

The relationship between advertising and other IMC components creates powerful synergies. PR efforts gain more traction when they're promoting something people have already seen advertised — the familiarity makes the coverage more meaningful. Direct marketing becomes more effective when it references advertising themes the recipient already recognizes. Promotions gain legitimacy when they're presented as natural extensions of advertised brand promises rather than random discounts. And digital channels provide endless opportunities to extend advertising messages into deeper engagements through clickable ads, shareable content, and interactive experiences.

Crafting advertising for integration requires thinking beyond the single ad or campaign. Every commercial, banner ad, or sponsored post should be conceived as part of a larger ecosystem of communication. The visuals should align with how the brand appears in PR materials and on digital platforms. The tone of voice should match how customer service representatives speak and how social media managers engage. The messaging should complement rather than contradict what's being said through other channels. This consistency doesn't mean every ad must look and sound exactly the same — different platforms require different adaptations — but they should all feel unmistakably like they come from the same brand with the same core identity.

Measurement in integrated advertising also takes a broader view. Instead of just tracking impressions or click-through rates, successful IMC evaluates how advertising contributes to larger business goals and how it works with other components to move customers through the buying journey. A TV spot might not generate immediate clicks, but if it increases search volume for branded terms that then convert through digital channels, that's a win. A social media ad might not lead directly to sales but could prime audiences to respond better to subsequent email campaigns. This holistic view of advertising effectiveness is what separates IMC from traditional approaches.

The best integrated advertising also leverages data from other channels to become more relevant and targeted. Insights from direct marketing campaigns can inform advertising creative. Social media listening can reveal what messaging resonates most with different audience segments. Website analytics can show which value propositions deserve more emphasis. This continuous feedback loop ensures advertising stays aligned with what audiences actually care about rather than what marketers assume they care about.

Adaptability is another crucial aspect of advertising in IMC. Unlike traditional campaigns that might run unchanged for months, integrated advertising often evolves in real time based on how other components are performing. If a PR crisis emerges, advertising can pivot to address concerns. If a particular promotional offer gains unexpected traction, ads can shift to highlight it more prominently. If certain digital channels show particularly strong engagement, ad budgets can be reallocated to capitalize on that success. This fluid approach requires close coordination across teams but results in far more effective communication overall.

Storytelling remains at the heart of great advertising, but in an IMC context, the story doesn't end with the ad — it continues across other touchpoints. A compelling narrative started in a commercial can be expanded through PR coverage, deepened through direct marketing content, activated through promotions, and discussed endlessly through digital channels. This multiplatform storytelling creates richer brand experiences that simple standalone advertising could never achieve.

The visual language of advertising also plays a critical role in integration. Consistent use of colors, fonts, imagery styles, and design elements across all ads makes them instantly recognizable as part of the brand family. When these same visual cues appear in PR materials, on packaging, in emails, and across digital platforms, they create a cohesive brand world that feels familiar no matter where customers encounter it. This visual consistency builds trust and makes all communications more effective through the power of repetition and recognition.

Budgeting for advertising within IMC requires considering how each dollar spent will amplify and be amplified by other activities. Rather than allocating separate budgets to different channels and formats, integrated approaches often pool resources to ensure advertising works in concert with other initiatives. A smaller but well-coordinated advertising spend that's perfectly timed with PR pushes and promotional periods often outperforms larger but isolated campaigns.

The human element remains vital even in our increasingly digital advertising world. Behind every data point and algorithm are real people making emotional connections with brands. Integrated advertising succeeds when it speaks to human needs, desires, and aspirations in ways that feel authentic across every platform. Whether through humor, inspiration, practical help, or sheer creativity, ads that touch people emotionally create the strongest foundations for integrated campaigns.

As media fragmentation continues and attention spans shorten, the challenge of creating advertising that cuts through the noise while maintaining integration with other communications only grows. The solution lies not in shouting louder but in speaking more meaningfully — crafting messages so relevant and valuable that people want to engage with them across multiple touchpoints. This is the essence of advertising in integrated marketing communications: not just making ads, but creating connected brand experiences that begin with advertising and ripple outward through every other communication channel.

Public Relations in Integrated Marketing Communications

Public relations represents the authentic voice of a brand in the marketplace - not what companies say about themselves through paid advertising, but what others say about them through earned media and organic conversations. In an integrated marketing strategy, PR serves as the credibility engine that transforms corporate messaging into newsworthy stories, turning brand promises into third-party validated truths. Unlike advertising's controlled environment, public relations thrives in the unpredictable world of media relations, influencer engagement, and public perception, making it both the most powerful and most delicate component of IMC.

The magic of PR in an integrated approach lies in its ability to create ripple effects across all other communication channels. A well-placed feature article lends credibility to advertising claims. A thought leadership piece provides substance for social media discussions. A positive product review gives sales teams powerful talking points. When PR operates in isolation, these benefits remain limited, but when strategically coordinated with advertising, digital, and direct marketing efforts, the amplification effect can be extraordinary. Imagine a new product launch where media coverage begins building anticipation just as targeted ads start appearing, followed by social media engagement from influencers who received early samples - this is PR working in concert with other elements rather than as a separate activity.

Modern public relations has evolved far beyond the traditional press release distribution of the past. Today's PR professionals must be equal parts storytellers, data analysts, and crisis managers, capable of identifying emerging trends, shaping narratives across multiple platforms, and responding to public sentiment in real-time. The most effective PR strategies in IMC don't just seek media placements but create shareable content, cultivate relationships with key opinion leaders, and monitor brand conversations across both traditional and digital channels. This expanded role makes PR more measurable and impactful than ever before, moving from vague notions of "good publicity" to concrete metrics about how earned media drives business objectives.

The relationship between PR and advertising in IMC deserves special attention. While advertising delivers controlled, paid messages, PR generates organic, earned coverage - and when these work together strategically, they create a powerful one-two punch. Advertising can prime audiences to recognize and value PR coverage, while PR can validate and enhance advertising messages. For example, a healthcare company might run ads about its innovative new treatment while simultaneously placing stories in medical trade publications and arranging interviews with its researchers - the combination builds both awareness and credibility in ways neither could achieve alone.

Crisis communication represents one of PR's most critical contributions to integrated marketing. In today's hyper-connected world, negative news spreads faster than ever, and disjointed responses can escalate problems dramatically. An effective IMC approach ensures crisis communications align perfectly with advertising pauses, social media responses, and customer service protocols. The PR team's ability to craft quick, authentic, and consistent messaging across all touchpoints often determines whether a crisis becomes a minor setback or a brand-damaging event. This requires advance planning and cross-functional coordination that only integrated marketing can provide.

Thought leadership has emerged as another key PR function within IMC strategies. By positioning company executives as industry experts through bylined articles, speaking engagements, and media interviews, PR builds brand authority that makes all other marketing efforts more effective. This earned credibility makes advertising claims more believable, gives social media content more substance, and provides valuable material for sales teams and direct marketing efforts. The integrated approach ensures thought leadership initiatives support current campaigns and business objectives rather than operating as separate vanity projects.

Event marketing illustrates how PR creates tangible experiences that amplify other communication channels. A well-executed product launch event generates media coverage, social media buzz, attendee testimonials, and visual content that can be repurposed across advertising and digital platforms. The PR team's ability to create newsworthy moments gives the entire marketing effort authentic talking points that feel more genuine than manufactured advertising messages. Post-event, the photos, videos, and attendee reactions continue providing value across multiple channels in an ongoing integrated campaign.

The digital transformation has blurred traditional lines between PR and other marketing disciplines, creating both challenges and opportunities for integration. Social media platforms serve as hybrid spaces where PR, advertising, and customer service intersect. A single viral tweet might require coordinated responses from multiple departments - PR crafting the official statement, advertising adjusting campaign messaging, and social teams engaging directly with concerned customers. The brands that handle these situations best are those with strong IMC frameworks that break down silos between teams.

Measurement of PR effectiveness has grown increasingly sophisticated within integrated marketing. Beyond counting media clips and impressions, modern PR metrics assess how earned media contributes to lead generation, website traffic, and even sales conversions. By tracking how PR coverage interacts with other touchpoints in the customer journey - did the prospect read an article before clicking an ad? Did they search for the brand after seeing a news segment? - marketers can demonstrate PR's true business value. This data-driven approach helps justify PR investments and ensures activities align with overall marketing objectives.

Corporate social responsibility initiatives offer another area where PR contributes significantly to integrated efforts. Today's consumers expect brands to take stands on social issues, and PR plays the central role in communicating these commitments authentically. When CSR messaging aligns with advertising themes, employee communications, and digital content, it creates a cohesive brand identity that resonates with values-driven consumers. The PR team's ability to identify relevant causes and communicate participation effectively makes these efforts credible rather than appearing as shallow marketing ploys.

The media landscape's fragmentation requires PR professionals to be more strategic than ever in their outreach. A one-size-fits-all press release won't cut it when targeting trade publications, mainstream media, bloggers, and influencers across multiple platforms. Integrated PR tailors messages for each audience while maintaining core consistency with overall marketing themes. This might mean developing different angles on the same story for business, consumer, and industry media, or creating customized content packages for digital versus traditional outlets.

Employee communications have emerged as an increasingly important PR function within IMC. Engaged employees serve as powerful brand ambassadors, and PR ensures they receive consistent messaging they can share authentically through their personal networks. This internal alignment prevents the common disconnect between polished external marketing and confused staff members who can't articulate what their company stands for. When advertising campaigns launch, PR makes sure employees understand them first, creating a unified front across all brand interactions.

The rise of owned media channels has given PR new tools for integrated storytelling. Company blogs, podcasts, and video series allow brands to publish content directly to audiences while maintaining editorial quality that earns attention and respect. These owned channels complement earned media efforts and provide consistent messaging platforms that align perfectly with advertising campaigns. The best owned media strategies repurpose and amplify content across multiple formats - turning a CEO interview into blog posts, social quotes, and email newsletter content as part of an integrated content ecosystem.

Influencer relationships represent another area where PR contributes to integrated success. Unlike paid sponsorships (which fall more under advertising), genuine influencer engagement requires the relationship-building skills PR professionals excel at. Identifying the right influencers, cultivating authentic partnerships, and creating collaborations that feel organic rather than transactional all fall under PR's domain. When these influencer activities coordinate with advertising campaigns and promotional calendars, the combined impact far exceeds what each could achieve separately.

The integrated approach also transforms how PR handles routine announcements like executive appointments, financial results, or operational updates. Rather than treating these as obligatory disclosures, strategic PR looks for ways to connect them to larger brand narratives and marketing objectives. A new executive hire becomes an opportunity to reinforce company direction. A facility expansion demonstrates growth and commitment to communities. Quarterly earnings highlight innovations that matter to customers. This mindset ensures all communications contribute to cohesive brand building.

Local market activation shows how PR adapts global campaigns for regional relevance within an IMC framework. National advertising may establish broad awareness, but local media coverage, community events, and market-specific storytelling make the message resonate personally. PR professionals with grassroots understanding can identify the angles and channels that matter most in each location, creating connections that mass advertising alone cannot achieve. This localized layer completes the integration from broad awareness to personal relevance.

The storytelling power of PR makes it uniquely capable of creating emotional connections that complement advertising's more direct persuasion. While ads might highlight product features and benefits, PR can tell the human stories behind the brand - the researchers who developed the technology, the families whose lives were improved, the communities where the company makes a difference. These narratives give depth and meaning to marketing messages, creating the kind of emotional resonance that drives long-term brand loyalty rather than just short-term sales.

As media consumption habits continue evolving, PR's role in content strategy grows increasingly vital. The lines between journalism and content marketing blur, with PR professionals serving as bridges between brand messages and audience interests. By identifying topics that matter to both the company and its publics, PR creates opportunities for meaningful engagement across multiple platforms. This content then fuels owned media channels, social sharing, and even advertising retargeting in a continuous cycle of integrated communication.

The most successful brands approach PR not as a separate function but as the connective tissue that binds all marketing efforts together with credibility and authenticity. In an age of skepticism and information overload, consumers increasingly look past paid messages to seek third-party validation and peer recommendations. Public relations, when fully integrated with other marketing disciplines, provides this essential credibility while ensuring all brand communications tell one cohesive story. From shaping initial awareness to managing ongoing reputation to responding to crises, PR operates as both shield and amplifier for the entire marketing effort - making it not just another component of IMC, but perhaps its most vital one.

Direct Marketing in Integrated Marketing Communications

Direct marketing represents the precision instrument in the IMC toolkit – where broad awareness-building meets individualized conversation. Unlike mass advertising that speaks to crowds, direct marketing speaks to specific individuals by name, with messages tailored to their unique needs and behaviors. In an integrated strategy, direct marketing serves as the critical bridge between initial brand awareness and concrete customer action, combining the personal touch of one-to-one communication with the scalability of modern digital platforms.

The power of direct marketing in IMC comes from its ability to turn anonymous audiences into known individuals through progressive engagement. Imagine a potential customer who first encounters your brand through a television commercial, then receives a targeted email offering more information, followed by a personalized direct mail piece with a special offer. Each touchpoint builds on the last, creating a cohesive journey that feels intentional rather than random. This sequential approach transforms scattered impressions into meaningful relationships, with direct marketing providing the crucial links that move people from awareness to consideration to purchase.

Data forms the foundation of effective direct marketing within IMC. Every interaction – whether an email open, website visit, or purchase history – provides valuable information that refines future communications. But in an integrated approach, this data doesn't live in isolation. Insights from direct marketing campaigns inform advertising targeting, shape PR messaging, and guide promotional strategies. Conversely, data from other channels enhances direct marketing's precision. Perhaps social media engagement indicates growing interest in a particular product line, triggering a series of targeted emails to users who showed that interest. Or maybe PR coverage about a new service prompts follow-up direct mail to high-value customers who would benefit most. This continuous data flow between channels creates a marketing ecosystem that grows smarter and more effective over time.

Channel selection in direct marketing has expanded dramatically while maintaining its core purpose of direct response. Traditional mail pieces now coexist with email, SMS messaging, targeted digital ads, and even personalized video. The key in IMC isn't using every possible channel but selecting the right mix based on audience preferences and campaign objectives. A luxury brand might find high-touch direct mail more effective than bulk email, while a tech startup might prioritize in-app messages and behavioral email triggers. The unifying factor is that each channel carries consistent messaging adapted to its unique strengths, all working toward common business goals.

Message personalization represents direct marketing's superpower in integrated campaigns. Modern technology allows customization far beyond just inserting a name – we can tailor entire content streams based on past behavior, stated preferences, and predictive analytics. A retail brand might send different versions of the same campaign: one highlighting family-friendly products to parents, another featuring premium items to high-spending customers, each reflecting how those segments interact with the brand across all touchpoints. This level of personalization makes recipients feel understood rather than marketed to, increasing engagement and conversion rates.

Timing becomes especially crucial when direct marketing operates within an IMC framework. Sending a promotional email too early in the customer journey wastes the opportunity, while sending it too late misses the window of maximum interest. Integrated direct marketing uses signals from other channels to time communications perfectly. Did a prospect recently engage with your Instagram post about a new product? That might trigger an email with more details. Did they abandon a cart after seeing a retargeting ad? A timely SMS reminder could complete the sale. This orchestrated timing transforms isolated touches into a continuous conversation.

Lead nurturing demonstrates direct marketing's strategic value in IMC. Rather than making a single sales pitch, sophisticated programs guide prospects through multi-stage journeys with content tailored to their position in the buying cycle. Early-stage leads might receive educational content that builds trust, while sales-ready leads get product comparisons or limited-time offers. All this content aligns with broader campaign themes running in advertising and PR, creating a unified experience whether the prospect encounters the brand through earned, paid, or direct channels.

Testing and optimization give direct marketing its measurable advantage in integrated strategies. The ability to split-test subject lines, offers, creative elements, and timing provides concrete data about what works best with different audience segments. These insights don't just improve future direct marketing – they inform creative decisions in advertising, messaging strategies in PR, and content approaches in digital channels. When a particular value proposition consistently outperforms in email tests, it likely deserves emphasis in other marketing efforts too.

Integration between direct marketing and sales teams creates another powerful synergy. Well-designed direct marketing programs don't just generate leads – they qualify and nurture them, providing sales teams with warmer prospects and richer context about each lead's interests and behaviors. This alignment prevents the common disconnect where marketing generates volumes of unqualified leads that frustrate sales teams. Instead, direct marketing becomes the helpful introduction that makes the sales conversation more productive.

Retention marketing shows how direct marketing extends beyond acquisition to build lasting customer relationships. Automated email sequences after purchases, personalized replenishment reminders, and exclusive member offers all reinforce the brand connection during the critical post-purchase period. When coordinated with advertising that reinforces brand values and PR that highlights customer success stories, these efforts transform one-time buyers into loyal advocates.

The rise of marketing automation has supercharged direct marketing's role in IMC. Sophisticated platforms now allow brands to create complex customer journeys that respond dynamically to individual behaviors across channels. A prospect who downloads a whitepaper might enter an educational email sequence, while one who attends a webinar receives different follow-up content. These automated workflows ensure timely, relevant communication at scale while maintaining the personal touch that makes direct marketing effective.

Direct marketing also plays a crucial role in bridging online and offline experiences. A retail store might use email receipts to encourage online reviews. A direct mail piece could drive traffic to an exclusive landing page. An event follow-up might include both an email and a printed thank-you note. These omnichannel connections create seamless brand experiences that acknowledge how customers naturally move between digital and physical touchpoints.

Measurement and attribution demonstrate direct marketing's concrete contribution to business goals. Advanced tracking now connects direct marketing touches to eventual conversions, showing how email campaigns, targeted offers, and personalized communications influence the customer journey. This data proves ROI while revealing which integration points deliver the most value – perhaps email nurtures leads that eventually convert through paid search, or direct mail drives online purchases from certain demographic groups.

Privacy considerations have become increasingly important in direct marketing's evolution. As consumers grow more concerned about data use, successful programs balance personalization with respect, providing clear value in exchange for information. Transparency about data collection and easy opt-out options build trust that makes recipients more receptive to messages. This ethical approach aligns with the brand reputation built through PR and advertising efforts.

The future of direct marketing in IMC points toward even greater integration and automation. Artificial intelligence now enables predictive personalization – anticipating customer needs before they articulate them. Internet of Things devices create new direct communication channels through smart home displays and connected cars. Blockchain technology may revolutionize customer data ownership and sharing. Through all these changes, the core principle remains: direct marketing at its best feels less like marketing and more like a helpful conversation between a brand and its customers.

When fully integrated with other marketing components, direct marketing transforms from a tactical sales tool to a strategic relationship-builder. It provides the measurable, actionable connections that turn broad awareness into concrete business results. In an era of fragmented attention and marketing skepticism, this ability to deliver the right message to the right person at the right time – and to do so as part of a cohesive brand experience across all touchpoints – makes direct marketing not just another channel, but the nervous system that connects all elements of integrated marketing communications.

Promotion in Integrated Marketing Communications

Promotion serves as the spark plug that ignites customer action within an integrated marketing strategy. While advertising builds awareness and PR establishes credibility, promotion provides the immediate incentive that converts interest into measurable response. In today's cluttered marketplace, strategic promotions cut through the noise by offering tangible value at precisely the right moment in the customer journey. But when executed as part of an IMC approach, promotions transcend simple price cuts to become powerful brand-building tools that reinforce positioning while driving short-term results.

The art of promotion in integrated marketing lies in balancing immediate impact with long-term brand equity. A luxury retailer might focus on exclusive access or value-added services rather than percentage discounts to maintain premium positioning. A grocery chain could tie savings to loyalty program engagement that builds lasting relationships. The most effective promotions feel like natural extensions of the brand promise rather than desperate attempts to boost sales. This requires careful coordination with advertising messaging, PR narratives, and digital channel capabilities to ensure consistency across all touchpoints.

Promotional strategy begins with understanding the different types of incentives and their roles in the marketing mix. Price promotions including discounts, coupons and flash sales create urgency for immediate purchases. Value-added promotions like bonus products or extended warranties enhance perceived worth without eroding price integrity. Experiential promotions such as contests or VIP events generate excitement and social sharing. Loyalty programs encourage repeat business through points and tiered rewards. Each type serves different objectives within the customer journey, and an integrated approach selects the right mix based on campaign goals rather than defaulting to blanket discounts.

Timing represents one of promotion's most powerful yet often overlooked aspects in IMC. A well-planned promotional calendar aligns with advertising flights, PR announcements, product availability, and seasonal demand patterns. Back-to-school promotions gain impact when supported by targeted ads and educational content. Holiday specials perform better when coordinated with gift guide placements and social media gift ideas. Even routine promotions gain lift when timed to capitalize on external events like tax refund seasons or weather patterns. This synchronization creates multiple reinforcing touchpoints that make promotions feel timely and relevant rather than random or excessive.

Channel integration transforms good promotions into great ones. A print coupon becomes more redeemable when also available digitally. An in-store promotion gains awareness through geo-targeted mobile ads when customers are nearby. An online flash sale gets extended reach through influencer partnerships. The most successful modern promotions flow seamlessly across physical and digital environments, recognizing that customers engage with brands through multiple simultaneous touchpoints. This requires breaking down traditional silos between trade marketing, e-commerce, and brand teams to create unified experiences.

Creative execution elevates promotions from transactional to transformational. Instead of generic "20% off" messages, integrated promotions tell stories that connect emotionally. A sporting goods brand might tie discounts to local team achievements. A pet food company could connect donations to each purchase. These creative hooks make promotions memorable and shareable while reinforcing brand values. When the creative approach aligns with advertising campaigns and PR narratives, the combined effect amplifies impact across all marketing efforts.

Measurement and optimization separate strategic promotions from guesswork. Beyond tracking redemption rates, integrated programs analyze how promotions influence customer lifetime value, brand perception, and cross-category purchasing. Sophisticated attribution models reveal how promotions interact with other marketing elements - did customers see an ad before redeeming? Did PR coverage boost promotion awareness? This data informs future promotional planning and resource allocation across the entire marketing mix.

Technology has revolutionized promotional capabilities within IMC strategies. Mobile wallet integration enables seamless redemption without paper coupons. Dynamic pricing algorithms optimize discount levels in real time based on demand. AI-powered recommendation engines suggest personalized promotional bundles. These technological advances allow promotions to become more targeted, more measurable, and more integrated with other marketing systems than ever before. The brands winning today are those leveraging these tools to deliver the right offer to the right customer through the right channel at the right time.

Legal and ethical considerations form a critical component of promotional planning. Regulatory requirements vary by region and industry governing everything from contest rules to discount disclosures. Brand reputation considerations should guide promotional decisions - deep discounts might move product but damage premium positioning, while certain partnership promotions could alienate core customers. An integrated approach evaluates promotions not just for immediate sales impact but for long-term brand health and customer relationships.

Trade promotions represent a specialized area requiring particular integration finesse. Manufacturer promotions to retailers and distributors must align with consumer-facing efforts to create push-pull synergy. Coordinated timing ensures retail displays appear when advertising drives store traffic. Joint business planning aligns trade incentives with brand-building objectives. This B2B/B2C integration prevents the common disconnect where trade promotions generate inventory that languishes without consumer demand.

Loyalty programs have evolved into sophisticated promotional platforms that blend instant gratification with long-term engagement. The best programs integrate across all customer touchpoints - recognizing in-store purchases in the mobile app, offering online exclusives to high-tier members, and providing personalized offers based on full purchase history. These programs generate valuable data that enhances all marketing efforts while creating ongoing reasons for customers to choose your brand repeatedly.

Social media has transformed promotional execution by adding viral potential and real-time interaction. User-generated content contests, limited-time Instagram offers, and Twitter-exclusive deals create buzz while driving measurable response. The integration challenge lies in maintaining brand consistency across these participatory promotions while meeting platform-specific expectations. Successful social promotions feel native to each channel while clearly connecting to broader campaign themes.

Experiential promotions create memorable brand interactions that transcend traditional discounting. Pop-up installations, interactive demonstrations, and sampling events provide tangible brand experiences that generate organic word-of-mouth. When these experiences are amplified through PR coverage, social sharing, and follow-up digital engagement, they create promotional impact that lasts far beyond the event itself. The integration comes from ensuring every element - from staff training to hashtag campaigns - reflects consistent brand messaging.

Personalization represents the future of promotional effectiveness. Instead of mass discounts, targeted offers based on purchase history, browsing behavior, and predicted needs increase relevance while protecting margins. This requires integrating promotional systems with customer data platforms to enable real-time decisioning. A hotel chain might offer spa upgrades to guests who previously booked them, while a retailer suggests complementary products to past purchasers. These tailored promotions feel considerate rather than pushy, building relationships while driving incremental sales.

Budget allocation for promotions within IMC requires strategic prioritization. Rather than spreading funds thinly across many small offers, integrated approaches concentrate investment on high-impact programs that align with business objectives. A new product launch might warrant aggressive introductory promotions, while established items focus on loyalty-building incentives. This disciplined approach prevents promotional fatigue while maximizing return on marketing investment across all channels.

The psychology behind promotional response offers valuable insights for integrated planning. Scarcity triggers like limited quantities or time windows create urgency. Social proof from showing popular choices influences decisions. The endowment effect makes customers value products more once they "own" them through trials or samples. Understanding these behavioral principles helps craft promotions that work with - rather than against - natural decision-making processes across all marketing touchpoints.

Global brands face particular challenges in promotional integration across markets. Currency fluctuations, cultural norms, and regulatory environments all impact what promotions work where. An integrated approach develops core promotional frameworks that maintain global brand consistency while allowing local adaptation. A "buy more, save more" structure might apply worldwide, but the discount thresholds, participating products, and supporting marketing would vary by region based on local market conditions.

Promotional innovation keeps brands ahead in competitive markets. Subscription models create predictable purchase cycles. Dynamic bundling suggests complementary products in real time. Gamification elements like progress bars or achievement badges increase engagement. These innovative approaches work best when integrated with broader marketing systems - subscription messaging aligns with CRM communications, dynamic bundles leverage product recommendation algorithms, and gamification elements appear consistently across app and web experiences.

The most effective promotional strategies view discounts and incentives not as necessary evils but as valuable tools for shaping customer behavior and reinforcing brand positioning. When promotions are planned as integral components of the marketing mix rather than last-minute sales tactics, they become powerful levers for achieving both short-term and long-term business objectives. In an increasingly crowded and price-sensitive marketplace, this strategic approach to promotion makes the difference between brands that discount their way to irrelevance and those that use promotions to build lasting customer relationships and sustainable competitive advantage.

Digital Channels in Integrated Marketing Communications

Digital channels have fundamentally transformed how brands communicate with their audiences, evolving from supplemental marketing tools to the central nervous system of modern IMC strategies. Unlike traditional media with its one-way broadcasts, digital platforms create dynamic, interactive ecosystems where brands and consumers engage in continuous dialogue. These channels don't just carry messages — they facilitate experiences, build communities, and generate real-time data that fuels every other component of integrated marketing. The true power of digital in IMC emerges when these channels stop operating as isolated silos and start functioning as interconnected parts of a living, breathing communication network that adapts and evolves with audience behavior.

The landscape of digital channels stretches far beyond websites and social media to encompass an ever-expanding array of touchpoints. Owned properties like branded apps and email lists provide controlled environments for direct engagement. Earned spaces including social conversations and online reviews offer authentic peer interactions. Paid opportunities such as search ads and influencer partnerships extend reach strategically. Shared platforms from e-commerce marketplaces to review sites present both challenges and opportunities for brand control. Each channel serves distinct purposes within the customer journey, but their real magic happens when coordinated to create seamless cross-channel experiences that feel personal rather than programmed.

Content sits at the heart of effective digital channel strategy within IMC. Unlike traditional advertising's campaign-based approach, digital demands an always-on content engine that delivers consistent value across platforms. A technology company might repurpose whitepapers into blog posts, infographics, webinar content, and social media threads—all conveying the same core messages in formats optimized for each channel. This content ecosystem ensures brand narratives develop depth and continuity rather than appearing as fragmented soundbites. The most sophisticated programs use content clusters—groups of interlinked pieces covering different angles of a topic—to dominate search results while providing comprehensive information that builds authority and trust.

Data integration represents digital's game-changing contribution to IMC. Every click, view, like, and share generates signals that refine audience understanding and campaign optimization. When this data flows freely between systems, remarkable synergies emerge—social media engagement metrics inform email segmentation, website behavior triggers personalized retargeting ads, and purchase history shapes content recommendations. This closed-loop intelligence allows brands to move beyond demographic targeting to true behavioral and intent-based marketing. The integration challenge lies in connecting these data streams while respecting privacy concerns and maintaining human-centric messaging that avoids creepy over-personalization.

Social media platforms exemplify the dual nature of digital channels as both broadcast mediums and community spaces. Brands must balance promotional messaging with authentic engagement, responding to comments, participating in trends, and sometimes navigating crises in real-time. The integration imperative here involves aligning social voice with overall brand positioning while adapting to each platform's unique culture — LinkedIn demands professional tone, TikTok rewards creativity, and Twitter thrives on timely reactions. Social listening tools bridge these channels with broader IMC efforts by surfacing audience insights that inform content calendars, advertising creative, and even product development.

Search marketing demonstrates how digital channels intersect with consumer intent in powerful ways. Search engine optimization (SEO) ensures owned content surfaces when audiences seek solutions, while paid search ads intercept commercial queries at decision moments. Integrated marketers coordinate these efforts with PR link-building strategies, social media discussions that drive search volume, and website experiences that convert visitors. Voice search and visual search innovations are expanding these opportunities, requiring content strategies that answer questions conversationally and optimize for emerging discovery methods.

Email marketing remains one of digital's most potent channels when executed as part of an IMC strategy. Far from batch-and-blast spam, modern email programs deliver hyper-personalized journeys that reflect individual behaviors across all touchpoints. A retail brand might send browsing abandonment emails featuring recently viewed items, follow-up with post-purchase care instructions, then nurture the relationship with loyalty program benefits—all while maintaining visual and messaging consistency with concurrent advertising campaigns. The deepest integration occurs when email systems share data with CRM platforms, ad networks, and POS systems to create truly unified customer profiles.

Emerging technologies continuously reshape digital channel possibilities. Conversational AI enables 24/7 customer dialogues through chatbots and voice assistants. Augmented reality brings products into customers' physical spaces virtually. Blockchain applications may revolutionize digital ownership and loyalty programs. Web3 concepts like NFTs and decentralized communities present new engagement frontiers. Forward-thinking IMC strategies test these innovations while grounding them in core brand objectives rather than chasing shiny objects for their own sake.

Measurement and attribution form digital channels' crown jewels for integrated marketers. Multi-touch attribution models reveal how combinations of touchpoints — a social ad impression plus an email open plus a search click — work together to drive conversions. Marketing mix modeling quantifies digital's contribution alongside traditional media. Real-time dashboards allow in-campaign optimization across channels. This analytical power enables data-driven decisions about where to invest for maximum impact, taking IMC from philosophical concept to scientific practice.

The human element remains vital amidst all this technology. Digital channels at their best facilitate genuine human connections at scale — the service rep who solves a problem via Twitter DM, the passionate brand community that forms on Discord, the educational creator who builds trust through YouTube tutorials. Integrated marketing succeeds when it leverages digital tools to enhance rather than replace these human experiences, ensuring technology serves brand-building rather than the reverse.

Looking ahead, digital channels will continue their rapid evolution, but certain principles endure for IMC success: consistency across touchpoints, adaptability to platform nuances, data integration that informs rather than overwhelms, and always putting audience value before brand promotion. The marketers who thrive will be those who view digital not as a separate discipline but as the connective tissue linking all communication efforts — the dynamic, measurable, interactive fabric of modern brand storytelling.

When fully integrated, digital channels transform from isolated tactics into a coordinated system that amplifies every other marketing element — giving advertising campaigns extended life through content repurposing, providing PR stories with measurable engagement, turning promotions into shareable experiences, and converting customer interactions into rich data that fuels continuous improvement. This holistic approach makes digital not just another channel, but the central nervous system of twenty-first century marketing communications.

Lesson 3: Building a Successful IMC Strategy

Creating an effective Integrated Marketing Communications strategy resembles conducting a symphony orchestra - every instrument must play its part at the right moment, guided by a shared vision, to create a harmonious performance that resonates with the audience. This process begins not with deciding what to say, but with deeply understanding who needs to hear it. The foundation of any successful IMC strategy lies in comprehensive audience insight that goes far beyond basic demographics to uncover the psychological and behavioral drivers that influence how people engage with brands across different touchpoints.

Understanding the Target Audience

Truly knowing your audience means moving past superficial categorizations to grasp their daily realities, unspoken anxieties, and aspirational dreams. It's about recognizing that a 35-year-old working mother experiences your brand differently at 7 AM when she's rushing to get kids ready for school versus 10 PM when she finally has time for herself. Modern audience understanding combines multiple research approaches - quantitative data reveals what people do, while qualitative insights explain why they do it. Social listening tools uncover unfiltered conversations, customer journey mapping identifies key decision points, and persona development transforms abstract data into relatable human profiles.

The most effective IMC strategies segment audiences not just by who they are, but by where they stand in their relationship with the brand. First-time visitors need different information than loyal customers. Price-sensitive shoppers require distinct messaging from those prioritizing quality. Geographic, cultural, and even weather-related factors can dramatically alter how audiences perceive and respond to communications. This multidimensional understanding informs every subsequent strategic decision, ensuring messages resonate rather than repel.

Psychographic profiling takes audience understanding even deeper by examining values, lifestyles, and personality traits. A sustainability-focused consumer will respond to different appeals than one motivated primarily by convenience or status. Behavioral economics principles help predict how audiences might react to various message framings or promotional structures. These psychological insights become particularly valuable when coordinating communications across channels, as they reveal the underlying consistencies that should permeate all touchpoints even as surface-level messaging adapts to different contexts.

The digital age has transformed audience understanding from static snapshots to dynamic, real-time portraits. Continuous feedback loops through social media interactions, website analytics, and customer service touchpoints allow brands to refine their understanding constantly. This living perspective prevents the common pitfall of developing strategies based on outdated assumptions while enabling messages to evolve alongside shifting audience needs and market conditions.

Defining the Core Message

With deep audience insight as the foundation, the next critical step involves distilling your brand's essence into a core message that's both flexible enough to adapt across channels and consistent enough to build recognition. This isn't about crafting a slogan, but rather identifying the central idea that all communications will express in various forms - the strategic "true north" that keeps every component aligned even as execution varies.

An effective core message balances aspiration with authenticity. It articulates not just what you sell, but why it matters in people's lives. For a financial services company, this might shift from "we offer low fees" to "we help you feel secure about tomorrow." For a fitness brand, it could transform from "high-quality equipment" to "your strongest self starts here." This higher-order benefit becomes the thread that weaves through advertising copy, PR narratives, social content, and all other communications.

Message architecture provides the structure for maintaining consistency while allowing necessary adaptation. Primary messages represent the unchanging brand pillars - the fundamental promises that remain reliable over time. Secondary messages support these pillars with proof points and product-specific details that may rotate based on campaigns or seasons. Tertiary messages include timely, contextual content that keeps communications fresh and relevant. This tiered approach prevents the common trap of either rigidly repeating the same phrases verbatim across channels or creating disjointed communications that share no common DNA.

Emotional resonance separates memorable core messages from forgettable ones. Neuroscientific research confirms that feelings drive decisions far more than facts alone. An IMC strategy that identifies the key emotions it needs to evoke - whether trust, excitement, belonging, or security - can then craft messages that elicit these feelings across different channels. A technology brand might inspire awe through cinematic ads while fostering community through user-generated social content, all tied to the same core message about human potential.

Strategic message testing prevents costly missteps before full campaign deployment. Focus groups, surveys, and digital A/B testing reveal how different audience segments interpret and respond to message variations. This validation process is especially crucial for global brands needing to ensure their core idea translates appropriately across cultures without losing its essence or accidentally offending. The most adaptable core messages work like musical themes - recognizable whether played by a full orchestra or a solo instrument.

Selecting Appropriate Channels

Channel selection in IMC resembles choosing the right utensils for a gourmet meal - each serves distinct purposes, and using the wrong one can spoil the experience. This decision-making process begins by mapping audience media consumption habits against campaign objectives to identify where and how to reach people most effectively. The goal isn't to be everywhere, but to be precisely where it matters with messages tailored to each environment.

Traditional mass media like television and print still play vital roles for broad awareness-building, particularly when targeting demographics that remain heavy consumers of these channels. However, their use in IMC strategies now focuses increasingly on driving audiences toward more personalized digital interactions rather than serving as standalone solutions. A TV spot might tease a storyline continued online, while a print ad directs readers to an augmented reality experience.

Digital channels offer unprecedented targeting precision but require careful selection to avoid wasteful fragmentation. Social platforms each attract distinct user behaviors - LinkedIn for professional networking, Instagram for visual inspiration, Twitter for real-time conversation. Programmatic advertising automates placement decisions based on audience data, while search marketing intercepts users at moments of explicit need. The integrated approach coordinates these digital touches to create cumulative impact rather than isolated impressions.

Emerging channels continually reshape the selection landscape. Voice search optimization becomes crucial as smart speaker adoption grows. Podcast sponsorships reach engaged niche audiences. Messaging apps enable conversational commerce. The IMC mindset evaluates these options not as shiny new objects but as potential puzzle pieces that could complete the customer journey when used strategically alongside established channels.

Budget allocation follows channel prioritization based on contribution to objectives. The 70-20-10 rule often applies - 70% of resources to proven performers, 20% to growing channels showing promise, and 10% to experimental innovations. This balanced approach maintains stability while allowing for evolution. Integrated planning tools help visualize how spend across channels works together to maximize reach and frequency without excessive overlap.

Timing coordination transforms individual channel efforts into cohesive campaigns. A product launch might begin with teaser social posts, followed by PR announcements, then targeted digital ads reinforcing key messages, all leading to retail promotions when interest peaks. This orchestrated sequencing ensures audiences encounter the brand multiple times through different lenses, with each exposure building on the last rather than repeating it verbatim.

Measurement frameworks must account for how channels interact rather than evaluating each in isolation. Multi-touch attribution models reveal how combinations of exposures drive conversions, while marketing mix modeling quantifies each channel's contribution to overall objectives. These insights feed continuous optimization, allowing resources to shift toward the highest-performing integrations as campaigns progress.

The most sophisticated IMC strategies incorporate both active channels where brands initiate communication and passive channels where they respond to audience-initiated interactions. This balanced approach recognizes that modern consumers move fluidly between discovering brands and seeking them out, between consuming content and creating their own. The channel mix must accommodate this dynamic, two-way engagement pattern to fully surround the customer journey.

By combining deep audience insight with a compelling core message and strategic channel selection, IMC strategies achieve that rare marketing alchemy where the whole becomes dramatically greater than the sum of its parts. The result isn't just coordinated communications, but cohesive brand experiences that feel simultaneously ubiquitous and personal - meeting audiences where they are with what they need, across every touchpoint, to build relationships that endure well beyond any single campaign.

Practical Exercise: Applying IMC Fundamentals to a Real Business

Let's take a local organic juice bar called "Green Revive" as our example business for this exercise. This small but growing chain of three locations wants to increase brand awareness and customer loyalty in their competitive urban market. Now, let's identify how each IMC component could work together to create a cohesive marketing strategy.

Advertising Components:

For Green Revive, visually striking out-of-home ads near fitness centers and yoga studios would establish brand presence where their health-conscious target audience spends time. Digital ads could target keywords like "healthy breakfast" and "cold-pressed juice," while social media ads might feature user-generated content of customers enjoying their vibrant drinks. The ads would all use the same color palette of fresh greens and yellows, with consistent messaging about "Real nutrition for real energy."

Public Relations Strategies:

The juice bar could position its founder as a nutrition expert available for local media interviews about wellness trends. A press release about their new zero-waste initiative would appeal to environmentally-focused publications. Partnering with a local fitness influencer for a "30-Day Green Challenge" could generate organic social buzz and potential news coverage about community health improvements.

Direct Marketing Tactics:

An email welcome series for new customers would share the brand story and nutritional benefits, while a loyalty program app could send personalized recommendations based on past purchases. Post-purchase SMS messages might ask for feedback and offer a discount on next visit. These direct communications would use the same friendly, expert tone as other brand touchpoints.

Promotional Activities:

Seasonal promotions like "Summer Hydration Packs" would align with weather changes when people seek refreshing options. A "Bring a Friend" Monday special drives weekly traffic during typically slow periods. All promotions would be supported by in-store signage matching the digital campaign assets, creating visual consistency across channels.

Digital Channel Integration:

The website would feature an interactive nutrition calculator using their ingredients, while Instagram would showcase mouthwatering product shots and behind-the-scenes footage of juice preparation. A YouTube series could demonstrate simple home recipes using their leftover pulp (tying into their sustainability story). All digital properties would link to their online ordering system and loyalty program signup.

Implementation Plan:

Month 1: Launch foundational elements (website refresh, loyalty program)
Month 2: Begin advertising and PR push around nutrition themes
Month 3: Introduce first seasonal promotion with full channel support
Ongoing: Social media engagement and email nurture sequences

Consistency Checks:

All materials would feature:

- The same vibrant fruit/vegetable photography style

- Common brand voice (friendly yet authoritative on nutrition)

- Unified call-to-action ("Start your green journey today")

- Matching color scheme and logo treatment

This integrated approach ensures whether a customer sees a billboard, gets an email, or visits the café, they experience the same core brand identity and messaging, just adapted appropriately for each channel and context. The exercise demonstrates how even a small business can develop a sophisticated IMC strategy by carefully coordinating these components.

Module 2: Aligning Messages Across Channels

Lesson 1: Consistency in Advertising Messages

Lesson 2: PR as Part of the IMC Strategy

Lesson 3: The Role of Digital Channels in Integration

Short Assignment

Module 2: Aligning Messages Across Channels

Imagine walking into a restaurant where the host greets you warmly, the menu descriptions make your mouth water, and the server recommends the perfect wine pairing—all working together to create one seamless dining experience. Now picture that same level of harmony in your marketing communications, where every channel speaks with the same compelling voice while playing its unique role. That's what this module is all about—the art and science of creating consistent yet channel-optimized messages that build brand recognition and trust across every touchpoint.

We've moved beyond the basics of IMC and now dive into the practical magic of message alignment. This is where strategy meets execution, where your core brand message learns to adapt without losing its soul. Today's consumers don't separate their experiences into "advertising," "PR," and "social media"—to them, it's all just "Brand X." When these touchpoints clash or contradict, confusion sets in. But when they reinforce each other through thoughtful alignment, they create marketing synergy that cuts through the noise of our oversaturated media landscape.

This module will show you how to craft messages that maintain their essence whether condensed into a tweet, expanded into a press feature, or visualized in a display ad. You'll learn why PR shouldn't operate in a silo but rather amplify your advertising themes, and how digital channels can extend your campaign's reach while providing real-time feedback to refine all other components. We'll explore the delicate balance between consistency and customization—how to sound unmistakably like your brand while respecting each channel's unique culture and audience expectations.

The businesses that get this right enjoy remarkable advantages. Their ads feel more credible because the claims are validated by PR coverage. Their social content sparks more engagement because it echoes themes from email campaigns. Their promotions convert better because the offers align with current brand storytelling. Most importantly, their customers develop clearer, stronger brand perceptions because every interaction builds on the last rather than starting from scratch.

By the end of this module, you'll be able to take one core message and adapt it authentically across multiple formats—a skill we'll immediately put to the test in our short assignment. You'll understand how to build campaigns where earned, owned, and paid media work together like sections of an orchestra, each playing distinct parts that combine into marketing harmony.

This isn't about rigid repetition—it's about strategic variation on a theme. Like a great song that sounds equally powerful whether performed as an acoustic ballad or electronic remix, your brand messages should maintain their essence while adapting to different contexts. That's the sweet spot we're aiming for—where consistency meets creativity, and integration amplifies impact.

Let's begin the work of making your messages sing together across every channel.

Lesson 1: Consistency in Advertising Messages

Picture your favorite brand for a moment. What comes to mind? The colors, the logo, the way their ads make you feel? That instant recognition doesn't happen by accident—it's the result of carefully crafted consistency across every advertising message. In today's fragmented media landscape where consumers encounter brands through countless touchpoints, maintaining this consistency isn't just helpful—it's essential for cutting through the noise and building lasting brand equity.

Creating coherent advertising messages starts with understanding that consistency doesn't mean repetition. It's not about using the same exact words everywhere, but about ensuring every piece of communication feels unmistakably like your brand while adapting appropriately to different contexts. Think of it like a person's personality—you're recognizably yourself whether you're at a business meeting, a family dinner, or a casual outing with friends, even though your behavior adjusts slightly for each situation. Your advertising needs that same flexible consistency.

The foundation of message coherence lies in developing a clear brand platform—a strategic document that articulates your brand's essence, personality, and key differentiators. This becomes the creative brief for all advertising efforts, ensuring every campaign builds on the same core identity. A sports apparel company might anchor all messages around "empowering everyday athletes," while a financial services firm could center on "making tomorrow less worrisome." These central ideas then manifest differently in a TV spot versus a social media post, but the underlying thread remains visible to consumers.

Visual consistency plays an equally crucial role in making advertising instantly recognizable. This goes beyond slapping your logo on everything—it's about developing a distinctive visual language that permeates all creative work. Consider Coca-Cola's signature red and dynamic ribbon, or Apple's clean minimalist aesthetic. These visual signatures transcend individual campaigns to create cumulative brand recognition. The key is developing design guidelines flexible enough to stay fresh but consistent enough to maintain identity—rules for color palettes, typography, image styles, and logo usage that allow for creativity within boundaries.

Brand voice represents the verbal equivalent of visual identity—the distinctive personality that comes through in every word your brand utters. Is your tone friendly or authoritative? Playful or serious? Inspirational or practical? A skincare brand targeting teenagers will communicate differently than one catering to dermatologists, even if they're selling similar products. Documenting voice characteristics—with examples of what to do and what to avoid—helps copywriters maintain consistency across all advertising touchpoints.

Adaptation across media formats presents the real test of message consistency. A 30-second TV commercial allows time for emotional storytelling, while a social media ad might have just seconds to capture attention. The skill lies in conveying the same core message in these different contexts—perhaps the TV spot shows someone achieving their dreams with your product's help, while the social ad highlights a customer testimonial about that transformational experience. Both communicate the same brand promise through different lenses.

Cultural adaptation adds another layer of complexity for global brands. While maintaining core consistency, advertising messages often need localization to resonate across markets. A campaign about "freedom" might emphasize different aspects in different cultures—personal independence in individualistic societies, family security in collectivist ones. The most successful global advertising manages to feel both globally consistent and locally relevant through careful message architecture.

Consistency over time builds brand equity, but staying fresh requires evolution. The best advertising campaigns strike a balance—maintaining recognizable elements while introducing new creative expressions. Think of McDonald's consistently using joy and convenience as themes while updating executions to reflect current cultural moments. This approach prevents brand fatigue while accumulating recognition value.

Measurement provides the feedback loop to ensure consistency drives results. Brand tracking studies monitor whether advertising messages are strengthening desired associations. Digital analytics reveal which consistent elements (like certain colors or messaging frameworks) perform best across channels. This data informs refinements to creative strategies without sacrificing core consistency.

The human brain is wired to prefer the familiar — it processes consistent messages more easily and remembers them better. In advertising, this translates to better recall, stronger emotional connections, and ultimately, greater effectiveness. When every ad, across every channel, builds on the same foundational identity, they don't just deliver impressions — they build a brand world that consumers recognize, trust, and want to be part of.

Aligning with Brand Visuals and Voice

Visual and verbal identity form the twin pillars of recognizable advertising — the distinctive look and sound that make your brand instantly identifiable even before the logo appears. Developing these elements strategically, then applying them consistently across all advertising touchpoints, creates the visual and verbal shorthand that cuts through today's cluttered media environment.

Brand visuals begin with color psychology — selecting hues that not only stand out but communicate your brand essence. A financial institution might choose blue for trust, while an organic food brand leans into greens for natural associations. These primary colors, along with secondary and accent palettes, should appear consistently across all advertising materials to build subconscious recognition. Typography choices similarly convey personality — a tech startup might use sleek sans-serifs to appear modern, while a heritage brand could prefer serif fonts suggesting tradition.

Photography and illustration styles contribute equally to visual identity. A travel brand might use bright, high-contrast images to evoke excitement, while a meditation app could prefer soft-focus, muted tones for calm. The key is establishing guidelines for lighting, composition, and editing that make all visual content feel cohesively "on brand" whether it's a billboard or Instagram story.

Logo usage rules ensure your most recognizable asset always appears at its best. These guidelines cover clear space requirements, minimum sizes, placement preferences, and versions for different backgrounds. Consistent application prevents the logo from becoming distorted or lost in layouts — a surprisingly common issue that dilutes brand recognition over time.

Voice guidelines bring similar consistency to how your brand speaks. Is your language straightforward or sophisticated? Do you use contractions to sound approachable? What's your stance on jargon or humor? Documenting these preferences with examples creates a verbal blueprint for all advertising copy. A youth-oriented brand might adopt slang carefully to sound authentic without trying too hard, while a B2B company could balance technical precision with plain-English explanations.

Tone adaptation recognizes that while voice remains consistent, tone should shift appropriately for context—like speaking more formally in a financial services ad but more playfully in social content. Good guidelines define these tonal ranges so advertising feels appropriate to each situation while remaining recognizably on-brand.

The intersection of visual and verbal identity creates what some call "brand world"—the cohesive universe where all advertising lives. In this world, certain phrases pair with specific visual treatments to create signature brand moments. A sneaker company might always show products in motion with action-oriented copy, while a tea brand could consistently use steaming cup close-ups paired with soothing language. These distinctive combinations become advertising trademarks that consumers associate specifically with your brand.

Style guides codify all these elements into living documents that evolve with the brand while maintaining core consistency. The best guides aren't restrictive rulebooks but inspirational playbooks—showing the full range of creative possibilities within brand parameters. They include examples of great executions across media types, demonstrating how flexibility and consistency coexist.

Training ensures everyone who touches advertising—internal teams and external agencies alike—understands how to work within brand identity. Regular creative alignment sessions keep all partners on the same page as campaigns develop. Some brands even create digital asset management systems that make on-brand visuals and templates easily accessible to all creators.

Digital advertising poses unique consistency challenges with its myriad formats and character limits. Adapting visual identity to tiny mobile banners or verbal identity to constrained tweet copy requires disciplined prioritization of the most essential brand elements. Many brands develop specific digital sub-guidelines showing how core identity translates to these unique environments without getting lost.

The payoff for this rigorous consistency comes in brand recognition and trust. Consumers develop subconscious "mental shortcuts" for brands they know—the sight of a particular color combination or the sound of a familiar voice triggers immediate associations. In split-second attention battles, these shortcuts give consistent advertisers a huge advantage. More importantly, they build the kind of familiarity that breeds trust—and trust remains advertising's most valuable currency.

Ultimately, consistent advertising isn't about limiting creativity but channeling it strategically. Like a great musician who develops a distinctive style while still creating fresh work, the most effective brands maintain recognizable identities while continuing to innovate. They understand that in a world of endless choices, consistency becomes the handshake that turns first-time buyers into lifelong customers.

Lesson 2: PR as Part of the IMC Strategy

Public relations represents the credibility engine of integrated marketing communications – the force that transforms brand messages into trusted stories through third-party validation. Unlike advertising's paid persuasion, PR earns attention by crafting narratives that media outlets, influencers, and communities want to share. When properly integrated, PR doesn't operate in a silo but amplifies and authenticates messages across all marketing channels, creating a powerful multiplier effect that money can't buy.

How PR Supports the Overall Strategy

PR's greatest contribution to IMC lies in its ability to make brand messages more believable. Consumers have grown skeptical of advertising claims but still trust earned media coverage. A product feature in a reputable publication carries more weight than a paid ad saying the same thing. Smart integration means PR and advertising teams work in tandem – advertising builds awareness of messages that PR then validates through independent sources. This one-two punch proves particularly effective when launching new products or entering competitive markets where credibility matters most.

Strategic storytelling forms the bridge between PR and other marketing components. While advertising highlights product benefits, PR crafts the larger narrative about why those benefits matter in people's lives or society. A home security company's ads might emphasize system features, while its PR team places stories about how the technology helps single parents feel safer – narratives that make the advertising claims more emotionally resonant. These stories then provide content for social media, email campaigns, and sales materials, creating an integrated content ecosystem.

Thought leadership represents another critical PR contribution to IMC strategies. By positioning company executives as industry experts through bylined articles, speaking engagements, and media interviews, PR builds authority that makes all marketing communications more persuasive. A financial services firm's ads about retirement planning gain impact when its CEO regularly comments in business media about economic trends. This earned credibility flows through to digital channels too – a LinkedIn post from an established thought leader gets more engagement than generic corporate content.

Crisis management showcases PR's protective role in integrated strategies. When negative situations emerge, coordinated response across all channels prevents mixed messages that could escalate problems. PR leads development of holding statements and Q&A documents that align with advertising pauses, social media responses, and customer service protocols. Brands with strong IMC frameworks can activate these crisis plans immediately, while those operating in silos often stumble with delayed or contradictory communications that damage reputation.

Community building has become PR's expanding frontier in integrated marketing. Rather than just broadcasting messages, modern PR cultivates genuine relationships with stakeholders through ongoing engagement. A pet food brand might sponsor adoption events that generate local media coverage while creating shareable content for social platforms and inspiring employee volunteerism that boosts internal morale. These community connections generate organic word-of-mouth that paid media alone cannot buy.

PR Tools: Press Releases, Events, Reputation Campaigns

Press releases remain foundational PR tools but have evolved far beyond dry announcements. Integrated marketing transforms releases into multimedia story packages – combining traditional text with embeddable videos, infographics, and social media assets that journalists can easily repurpose. A product launch release might include demo footage for TV stations, high-res images for print publications, and tweet-ready statistics for digital outlets. This approach increases pickup rates while ensuring consistent messaging across earned media placements.

Strategic timing aligns press releases with broader campaign calendars. Issuing a release about store expansions just as new location-specific ads debut creates geographic synergy. Announcing executive promotions alongside leadership-themed content campaigns reinforces the narrative. The most integrated PR teams maintain visibility into marketing schedules to identify these alignment opportunities rather than operating on separate timelines.

Media relations in an IMC context focus on creating mutual value rather than just pitching stories. PR professionals develop deep understanding of journalists' beats and audiences to provide truly relevant content. A food brand might share proprietary consumer research about dining trends with lifestyle editors, knowing the resulting coverage will mention their expertise while supporting broader marketing themes about changing eating habits. These relationships become especially valuable when needing to balance paid and earned media during intensive campaigns.

Brand events showcase PR's ability to create tangible experiences that fuel integrated marketing. Product launch parties, anniversary celebrations, or community initiatives generate multiple content streams – live social coverage, post-event recaps, media interviews, and visual assets that appear across channels. A well-designed event considers all these content needs upfront, with photo backdrops optimized for Instagram, talking points that echo advertising themes, and signage that reinforces visual identity. The most successful events feel like organic brand expressions rather than staged marketing moments.

Reputation campaigns represent PR's long-term strategic contribution to brand equity. While advertising drives immediate awareness, PR builds enduring credibility through sustained initiatives. A technology company might sponsor independent research about digital wellness, earning media coverage while establishing its products as part of the solution. A clothing retailer could partner with sustainable cotton initiatives, creating ongoing stories about environmental commitment. These campaigns provide content for years rather than just single news cycles.

Influencer engagement has blurred traditional lines between PR and marketing. Rather than just celebrity endorsements, strategic PR identifies authentic voices whose audiences align with brand goals – industry experts, niche content creators, or passionate customers. These relationships often begin with PR-style outreach focused on shared values rather than transactional sponsorships. When an influencer's organic praise aligns with paid campaign messaging, the combined effect far exceeds what either could achieve alone.

Corporate social responsibility (CSR) initiatives offer prime opportunities for PR to demonstrate brand values in action. Well-communicated CSR programs generate positive coverage while differentiating from competitors. An integrated approach ensures these initiatives connect to broader marketing themes – a water filter company supporting clean water access projects, or a children's brand advocating for play-based learning. PR then amplifies these efforts through multiple channels, turning goodwill into tangible brand attributes that consumers remember.

Employee advocacy programs leverage PR principles internally to turn staff into brand ambassadors. When employees understand and believe in company narratives, they share them authentically through personal networks. PR teams equip staff with social media content, talking points, and visual assets that maintain brand consistency while allowing personal expression. This organic reach complements paid efforts while adding human credibility that corporate channels can't replicate.

Measurement has evolved from simple clip counts to sophisticated analysis of PR's role in integrated performance. Advanced tools track how media coverage influences web traffic, search volume, and even sales conversions. Marketing mix modeling quantifies PR's contribution alongside paid media, while sentiment analysis assesses impact on brand perception. These metrics prove PR's business value while informing optimization of future integrated efforts.

The most effective PR in IMC strategies operates as both megaphone and listening ear – amplifying key messages while bringing audience insights back to inform marketing decisions. This two-way flow ensures all communications stay relevant and responsive rather than just broadcasting predetermined talking points. When PR truly integrates with other disciplines, it doesn't just support marketing goals but elevates entire brand perceptions in ways that create lasting competitive advantage.

In today's skeptical, information-saturated environment, consumers increasingly seek authentic connections with brands that stand for something beyond their products. Public relations, when fully integrated into marketing strategies, provides the credibility and depth that transforms transactions into relationships. From shaping initial awareness to managing ongoing reputation to navigating inevitable challenges, PR isn't just another communication channel – it's the foundation upon which enduring brands are built.

Lesson 3: The Role of Digital Channels in Integration

Digital channels have become the central nervous system of modern integrated marketing, connecting all other components into a living, breathing communication network. Unlike traditional media's one-way broadcasts, digital platforms create dynamic ecosystems where brands and consumers engage in continuous dialogue. These channels don't just carry messages — they facilitate experiences, build communities, and generate real-time data that fuels every aspect of an IMC strategy. The true power emerges when digital stops operating as isolated tactics and starts functioning as the connective tissue binding advertising, PR, promotions and direct marketing into seamless brand experiences.

Social Media: The Conversation Hub

Social platforms serve as the town squares of digital integration — spaces where paid, earned and owned media intersect organically. A single viral tweet can spark PR coverage that advertising then amplifies, while user-generated content provides authentic material for all channels. The integration magic happens when social listening informs campaign development, when trending topics inspire real-time content adaptations, and when community engagement provides continuous feedback to refine other marketing efforts.

Each platform demands distinct approaches while maintaining brand consistency. LinkedIn fosters professional thought leadership that supports B2B marketing goals. Instagram's visual nature showcases products in lifestyle contexts that echo advertising themes. Twitter's real-time conversations allow brands to insert themselves into cultural moments in ways that feel organic rather than forced. TikTok's creative freedom inspires viral challenges that can be repurposed across channels. The common thread is developing platform-specific content that still clearly communicates core brand messages.

Social commerce has blurred lines between engagement and conversion. Shoppable posts link directly to e-commerce while maintaining the social experience. Live shopping events combine entertainment with instant purchasing. These innovations require tight integration between marketing creative and backend systems — ensuring product availability, pricing and promotions stay synchronized across all touchpoints. Nothing breaks trust faster than a social promotion for an out-of-stock item.

Community management transforms social from megaphone to dialogue. Responding to comments, addressing concerns and celebrating user content builds relationships that traditional advertising can't replicate. These interactions generate qualitative insights about customer perceptions that can reshape broader campaign strategies. A surge of questions about product features might indicate needed clarifications in advertising. Repeated compliments about specific benefits should be highlighted across all communications.

Email Marketing: The Personalization Powerhouse

Email remains the workhorse of digital integration—the channel where broad awareness converts to individual relationships. Modern email programs have evolved far beyond generic blasts to become sophisticated behavioral trigger systems. A retail brand might send browsing abandonment emails featuring viewed items, follow up post-purchase with care instructions, then nurture the relationship with loyalty rewards—all while maintaining visual and voice consistency with concurrent ad campaigns.

Segmentation represents email's superpower in IMC strategies. Rather than one-size-fits-all messages, behavioral data allows hyper-relevant content streams. Frequent buyers receive different messaging than lapsed customers. Geographic targeting ensures weather-appropriate product recommendations. Purchase history informs personalized cross-sell suggestions. This precision makes email the ideal channel for bridging mass awareness campaigns with individual customer experiences.

Automation workflows turn email into an always-on engagement engine. Welcome series introduce brand narratives to new subscribers. Milestone emails celebrate customer anniversaries. Replenishment reminders drive repeat purchases for consumable products. These automated touches maintain relationships between major campaigns while requiring minimal ongoing effort—the ultimate integration of efficiency and personalization.

Testing culture maximizes email's contribution to integrated learning. Subject line A/B tests reveal which message framings resonate best. Send time experiments identify optimal engagement windows. Content variations determine which product benefits matter most to different segments. These insights don't just improve email performance — they inform messaging across all channels, creating a virtuous cycle of refinement.

Paid and Owned Content: The Digital Ecosystem

Paid digital advertising provides the scalable reach that complements owned media's depth. Social ads, search marketing and programmatic display work together to intercept audiences at multiple touchpoints along their journey. Retargeting brings back visitors who didn't convert, while lookalike audiences expand reach to new prospects resembling best customers. The integration art lies in coordinating these paid efforts with organic activities for maximum synergy.

Search marketing exemplifies digital integration at its best. SEO-optimized owned content answers questions audiences are actively asking, while paid search ads capture commercial intent at decision moments. PR link-building boosts domain authority that improves organic rankings. Together, these efforts ensure brands appear when and where it matters most — with messaging tailored to each stage of the buyer's journey.

Content marketing builds the owned assets that fuel integrated campaigns. Blogs, videos, tools and resources provide value beyond products while establishing brand authority. A financial services firm might create retirement planning calculators that both attract organic search traffic and provide sales teams with conversation starters. These assets can be repurposed across email nurtures, social posts and even traditional advertising — maximizing ROI on content investments.

Marketing technology stacks enable the data flows that make digital integration possible. Customer data platforms unify information from all touchpoints. Marketing automation systems trigger personalized journeys. Analytics tools measure cross-channel impact. When these technologies share data seamlessly, they create the single customer view that powers truly integrated experiences — where an ad click informs email content which shapes sales conversations.

The brands winning in digital integration treat their channels as interconnected parts of a whole rather than isolated silos. They understand customers move fluidly between social, email, search and websites — and design experiences that feel continuous rather than disjointed. They leverage each channel's unique strengths while maintaining unmistakable brand consistency. Most importantly, they use digital's real-time feedback loops to constantly refine all marketing efforts based on what actually resonates with their audience.

This holistic approach transforms digital from just another tactic to the central nervous system of modern integrated marketing — the dynamic, measurable, interactive fabric connecting all communication efforts into cohesive brand experiences that adapt and grow with customer relationships over time.

Short Assignment: Unified Message Adaptation Across Channels

Brand Scenario:
Let's use "EcoSleep," a sustainable mattress company that uses organic materials and has a recycling program for old mattresses. Their core message: *"Rest deeply while keeping the planet healthy - the most sustainable sleep solution that doesn't compromise on comfort."*

1. Print Ad Adaptation (Eye-catching Visual Medium)
Headline: "Your Dreamiest Sleep Yet - 100% Guilt-Free"
Visual: A person sleeping peacefully on an EcoSleep mattress floating over a lush green forest
Body Copy:
"EcoSleep's revolutionary organic mattresses give you cloud-like comfort while keeping synthetic materials out of landfills. Our plant-based memory foam and natural latex provide perfect support, and when it's time to replace, we'll recycle every layer. Better sleep. Better planet. *Breathe easy tonight.*"
Call-to-Action: "Try for 100 nights risk-free - Visit EcoSleep.com"

2. Tweet Adaptation (Concise & Engaging)
🌱 Tired of choosing between comfort & sustainability?

Our organic mattresses:
☑ Plant-based memory foam
☑ 100% recyclable
☑ 365-night trial

Sleep soundly knowing your bed helps the planet dream bigger. #SustainableSleep

---

[Image: side-by-side of mattress in bedroom & recycling facility]

3. Press Article Adaptation (Newsworthy Angle)
Headline: "Local Mattress Company Pioneers Circular Economy Model for Sleep Products"

Lead Paragraph:

As consumers increasingly demand sustainable home goods, EcoSleep is redefining the mattress industry with its closed-loop recycling program. The company's innovative approach ensures that every component - from organic cotton covers to plant-based foams - can be fully repurposed at end-of-life, preventing thousands of mattresses from entering landfills annually.

Key Messages Incorporated:

- Highlights the recycling program (sustainability proof point)

- Mentions material innovation (comfort + eco-benefits)

- Includes trial period (risk reduction)

- Positions as industry leader (credibility)

Why This Works:

1. **Consistent Core:** All versions communicate sustainable comfort but adapt the emphasis based on channel purpose

2. **Visual Alignment:** Each format could use variations of the "nature + sleep" visual theme

3. **Channel Optimization:**

   o Ad focuses on emotional benefits + clear CTA

- o Tweet uses brevity + hashtags for discovery

- o Press release offers journalists substantive news hooks

    4. **Unified Voice:** Maintains approachable yet authoritative tone across all pieces

Bonus Integration Tip:
The press coverage could later be repurposed into:

- Customer testimonials for the website

- Social proof in email campaigns

- Retail signage ("As featured in...")

- Talking points for sales teams

This exercise demonstrates how one core message can flex across channels while maintaining recognizable brand DNA and strategic consistency.

Module 3: Effectively Managing Integrated Campaigns

Lesson 1: Setting KPIs

Lesson 2: Scheduling and Budget Allocation

Lesson 3: Managing Teams and Agencies

Hands-On Exercise

Module 3: Effectively Managing Integrated Campaigns

Imagine trying to conduct an orchestra where every musician plays from a different sheet of music, at their own tempo, with no conductor to bring them together. That's what managing marketing communications feels like without proper integration. Now that we've covered the *what* and *why* of IMC, this module focuses on the *how* — the practical realities of turning strategic vision into coordinated execution across teams, timelines, and budgets.

Running integrated campaigns is equal parts art and science — requiring the precision of a project manager, the analytical mind of a data scientist, and the diplomatic skills of a UN negotiator. Why? Because you're not just managing tasks and budgets, but aligning different departments (each with their own priorities), external agencies (each with their own approaches), and leadership teams (each with their own expectations). The difference between campaigns that feel effortlessly cohesive versus those that feel patched together comes down to the often invisible work of orchestration behind the scenes.

We'll start by cutting through the KPI confusion—moving beyond vanity metrics to identify the measurements that actually connect to business outcomes. You'll learn how to set goals that advertising, PR, and digital teams can collectively own rather than compete over. Then we'll tackle the puzzle of budgeting across channels, where strategic allocation matters more than total spend. The tools you'll discover help answer critical questions like: *Should we shift funds from print ads to influencer partnerships? How do we balance immediate sales activation with long-term brand building?*

Team dynamics take center stage in our third lesson, where we address the human side of integration—getting creatives, analysts, and executives speaking the same language. You'll learn the IMC manager's playbook for facilitating collaboration between internal teams and external agencies, turning potential turf wars into productive partnerships. The best ideas fail without buy-in, and we'll cover techniques for building alignment from the C-suite to the interns.

The module culminates in a hands-on exercise where you'll build an integrated campaign plan for a real-world scenario—making the tough calls on timing, resource allocation, and team coordination that separate theoretical strategies from executable ones. You'll leave not just understanding integration intellectually, but feeling confident in your ability to make it happen amid the messy realities of organizational politics, budget constraints, and last-minute changes.

This is where many marketers discover that integration isn't a destination but a daily practice — a set of disciplines that keep all communication efforts moving in harmony even when surprises arise. Because they always do. By mastering these management fundamentals, you'll be equipped not just to create campaigns, but to lead them with the clarity and adaptability today's complex marketing environment demands.

Ready to transform from strategist to conductor? Let's begin.

Lesson 1: Setting KPIs for Integrated Campaigns

Imagine you're planning a cross-country road trip. You wouldn't just get in the car and start driving randomly - you'd set checkpoints along the way to ensure you're heading in the right direction. That's exactly what KPIs do for your integrated marketing campaigns. They serve as your strategic checkpoints, helping you navigate the complex journey of connecting with your audience across multiple channels while staying aligned with your ultimate business destination.

The art of selecting the right KPIs begins with understanding that not all metrics are created equal. In today's data-rich environment, it's easy to drown in numbers - impressions, clicks, shares, opens, mentions - the list goes on. The challenge isn't finding data, but identifying which data points truly matter for your specific campaign goals and business objectives. This requires moving beyond surface-level vanity metrics that might look impressive in reports but don't actually drive business results.

Let's consider a common pitfall many marketers face - focusing solely on engagement metrics like social media likes or video views. While these can indicate content resonance, they don't necessarily correlate with business outcomes unless tied to deeper actions. An integrated campaign for a new product might generate millions of impressions, but if those impressions don't translate to website visits, lead generation, or ultimately sales, were they truly valuable? This is why the most effective KPIs connect directly to your customer journey and business objectives.

Aligning KPIs with business objectives requires starting with the end in mind. Are you launching a new product? Then trial sign-ups or sample requests might be your north star metric. Building brand awareness in a new market? Share of voice and brand lift studies become crucial. Driving customer retention? Repeat purchase rates and loyalty program engagement take priority. The key is mapping backward from your ultimate business goal to identify which marketing activities and metrics will best support that objective.

For integrated campaigns specifically, you need KPIs that reflect how different channels work together rather than operating in isolation. Consider a customer who sees your billboard (impressions), clicks a social media ad (engagement), reads an earned media article (time spent), then finally makes a purchase (conversion). Siloed measurement would credit only the last touchpoint, while integrated measurement reveals how each component contributed to the journey. This holistic view is essential for understanding your true marketing ROI.

The most sophisticated KPI frameworks incorporate both leading and lagging indicators. Leading indicators - like website traffic increases or social engagement spikes - provide early signals about campaign performance while there's still time to optimize. Lagging indicators - such as quarterly sales figures or market share - confirm whether those early signals translated to business impact. Tracking both gives you the complete picture of marketing effectiveness.

Behavioral KPIs often prove more valuable than attitudinal ones in integrated campaigns. While surveys can tell you what people say they think or intend to do, behavioral data shows what they actually do across touchpoints. Did they watch your video to completion? Click through from your email? Redeem the promo code from your direct mail piece? These concrete actions provide clearer performance signals than general awareness or sentiment measures.

Financial KPIs remain the ultimate yardstick for marketing effectiveness, but require careful interpretation. Customer acquisition cost (CAC) needs to be evaluated against customer lifetime value (LTV). Marketing-influenced revenue accounts for campaigns that nurture leads even if they don't close immediately. Return on marketing investment (ROMI) calculations should consider both short-term sales lifts and long-term brand building. The most effective marketers speak the language of business outcomes, not just marketing activities.

Channel-specific KPIs still have their place within an integrated framework, but should ladder up to shared objectives. Your social team might track engagement rate, your PR team media mentions, and your search team click-through rate - but all should connect to overarching goals like lead quality or brand perception. This prevents channel teams from optimizing for metrics that don't actually move the business forward.

The timing of KPI measurement deserves special attention in integrated campaigns. Some effects are immediate (direct response conversions), while others emerge over time (brand preference shifts). Setting appropriate evaluation windows prevents premature judgments about campaign effectiveness. A brand awareness initiative might need three months before showing measurable impact on search volume and inbound inquiries, for example.

Qualitative KPIs provide crucial context that numbers alone can't capture. Customer interviews, social listening insights, and sales team feedback reveal the "why" behind the metrics. Perhaps your click-through rates are high but conversions low because the landing page doesn't deliver on the ad promise. Or media coverage is extensive but focused on the wrong aspects of your product. These qualitative insights help you interpret quantitative data more accurately.

Competitive benchmarking adds another dimension to KPI evaluation. Your 5% conversion rate might seem strong until you learn competitors average 8%. Share of voice compared to competitors indicates whether your messaging is cutting through the noise. These relative metrics help assess whether adequate progress is being made in your market context.

The most effective KPI dashboards balance comprehensiveness with focus. While you might track dozens of metrics operationally, the executive view should highlight the 3-5 that truly matter for decision making. Visualization is key - a well-designed dashboard tells the performance story at a glance, making it easier for cross-functional teams to stay aligned on what's working and what needs adjustment.

Remember that KPIs should inspire action, not just measurement. Every metric you track should have clear implications for optimization. If a KPI can't potentially change your decisions or tactics, it's probably not worth measuring. This action-orientation is what separates performance measurement from mere reporting.

As you implement your KPI framework, expect to refine it over time. What seemed important at campaign launch might prove less relevant in practice, while unexpected metrics may emerge as key indicators. This evolution is normal - the goal isn't to set perfect KPIs from day one, but to develop a learning mindset that continuously improves your measurement approach based on real-world results.

Ultimately, great KPI strategy is about focus - identifying the vital few metrics that truly indicate marketing success for your specific business objectives, then using those insights to optimize your integrated campaigns for maximum impact. When done well, your KPIs become more than just numbers on a dashboard - they transform into a powerful navigation system guiding your marketing efforts toward genuine business results.

Lesson 2: Scheduling and Budget Allocation for Integrated Campaigns

Planning an integrated marketing campaign without proper scheduling and budget allocation is like trying to bake a cake by throwing all the ingredients into the oven at random times - you might end up with something edible, but it won't win any awards. The magic happens when each component is added at just the right moment, in precisely measured amounts, with careful attention to how flavors blend together. This lesson will teach you how to be the master chef of your marketing campaigns, combining timing and resources in ways that create maximum impact.

Campaign Planning Tools for Seamless Execution

Modern marketers have moved far beyond spreadsheets and sticky notes (though those still have their place). Today's campaign planning tools act as central nervous systems for your integrated strategy, keeping all teams and channels aligned. Visual timeline platforms like Gantt charts provide at-a-glance views of how advertising launches will sync with PR pushes and digital activations. These tools help answer critical questions: Should social media teasers start before the TV spot airs? How long after the press release should the email campaign hit inboxes?

Cloud-based collaboration platforms have revolutionized campaign planning by allowing real-time updates across departments. When the PR team lands an unexpected media opportunity, the digital team can immediately adjust content calendars, and the advertising group can amplify the coverage with paid support. This dynamic coordination prevents the all-too-common scenario where one hand doesn't know what the other is doing, leading to missed synergies or worse - conflicting messages going out simultaneously.

Content management systems with calendar integrations ensure all assets are ready when needed. Imagine setting automated reminders that the product photos for next month's campaign need final approval today because the ad agency requires two weeks for production, while the social team needs them in different formats by Friday. These workflow tools prevent last-minute scrambles that compromise quality.

Budget tracking features integrated with planning tools provide real-time visibility into spending across channels. Rather than waiting for monthly reports, you can see immediately if paid search is underperforming so you can reallocate funds to better-performing social ads. Some advanced systems even incorporate AI recommendations for optimization based on performance data.

The Art and Science of Budget Allocation

Dividing your marketing budget across channels isn't about equal shares - it's about strategic investment where it will yield the highest returns. The 70-20-10 rule offers a helpful starting framework: 70% to proven performers, 20% to growing channels showing promise, and 10% to experimental innovations. But even this needs customization based on your specific campaign goals and audience behaviors.

Paid media often consumes the largest portion, but the most effective allocations consider how paid, owned, and earned media work together. That might mean reducing traditional ad spend to fund content creation that earns organic reach and backlinks, ultimately improving your SEM performance. Or shifting some social budget to influencer partnerships that generate both immediate conversions and long-term credibility.

Timing dramatically impacts budget effectiveness. A travel company would allocate heavily to search and social during booking seasons but shift to brand-building display ads during planning periods. B2B marketers might concentrate budgets around trade shows and quarterly sales pushes. This rhythmic spending aligns with customer decision cycles rather than spreading funds thinly year-round.

Testing budgets should be protected fiercely. The companies that stay ahead consistently dedicate portions of their budget to trying new platforms, formats, and messaging approaches. While not every test will succeed, those that do can become your next high-performing channels before competitors catch on.

Prioritizing Across Channels with Precision

The channel prioritization matrix is every IMC manager's secret weapon. By plotting channels against two axes - impact on objectives and efficiency of spend - you create a visual guide for resource allocation. High-impact, high-efficiency channels get the lion's share. High-impact but inefficient ones might receive targeted funding for strategic reasons. Low-impact options get minimized or eliminated, no matter how efficient.

Customer journey mapping informs these decisions. If analytics show your audience discovers products through social media but converts via email, you'd prioritize top-of-funnel social content and bottom-of-funnel email automation, with budget allocated accordingly. The middle-funnel consideration phase might blend retargeting ads and organic search content.

Competitive activity should influence but not dictate your allocations. If competitors dominate TV, maybe you counter with stronger digital presence. If they're ignoring an emerging platform relevant to your audience, that becomes your opportunity to own that space before prices rise.

The Integration Premium

Savvy budgeters always reserve 10-15% for integration costs - those often-overlooked expenses that make campaigns truly cohesive. This includes cross-channel analytics setups, asset adaptations for different platforms, and the crucial but invisible project management time required to keep everything aligned. Skipping this "glue budget" is why many campaigns feel disjointed despite having well-funded components.

Measurement and optimization budgets are equally vital. The ability to track performance across channels and quickly reallocate based on data often delivers higher ROI than the initial media spend itself. This includes funds for A/B testing, attribution modeling, and sometimes even small control groups to measure true incremental impact.

Agile Budget Management

The most successful marketers treat budgets as dynamic rather than fixed. Regular checkpoints (at least biweekly for intensive campaigns) should assess performance and allow for reallocation. Maybe the PR push is driving more web traffic than expected, warranting increased ad spend to capture that interest. Perhaps the podcast ads aren't performing, so those funds shift to high-converting search terms.

This agility requires having some budget held in reserve rather than fully committed upfront. The exact percentage varies by industry and campaign type, but 15-20% in flexible funds allows capitalizing on unexpected opportunities or doubling down on what's working.

Avoiding Common Budget Pitfalls

The "shiny object syndrome" tempts marketers to chase every new platform, but disciplined allocation requires saying no to good opportunities to focus on great ones. Similarly, the "we've always done it this way" trap keeps money flowing to traditional channels that may no longer deliver like they once did.

Equally dangerous is the "spend it or lose it" mentality that leads to rushed, wasteful Q4 expenditures. Better to have a plan for carrying over unused funds into special projects than to blow budgets on low-priority tactics just to hit spending targets.

Bringing It All Together

The companies that win at integrated marketing treat budget allocation as an ongoing strategic process rather than an annual exercise. They balance data-driven rigor with willingness to take calculated risks. They measure not just what each channel delivers individually, but how the combination performs synergistically. Most importantly, they remain flexible enough to shift as opportunities emerge and market conditions change.

When done well, strategic scheduling and budget allocation transform your marketing from a collection of tactics into a precision-engineered system where every dollar and every timeline decision amplifies the others. The result? Campaigns that don't just reach audiences, but resonate with them - delivering measurable business impact while building lasting brand value.

This disciplined approach to planning and spending separates marketing teams that simply execute tactics from those that drive genuine business growth. In the following hands-on exercise, you'll apply these principles to create your own integrated campaign plan, making the tough but rewarding decisions that turn strategy into reality.

Lesson 3: Managing Teams and Agencies for Integrated Campaigns

Picture the most complex orchestra you can imagine - string sections sitting with digital teams, brass players collaborating with PR specialists, percussionists syncing with social media managers. The IMC manager stands as the conductor of this diverse ensemble, ensuring all these talented professionals create marketing harmony rather than noise. This lesson reveals how to coordinate these moving parts to execute campaigns that feel effortlessly cohesive to your audience, no matter how many teams and agencies contribute behind the scenes.

Coordinating Internal Teams: Breaking Down Silos

The biggest obstacle to integrated marketing isn't lack of skill or resources - it's organizational silos. Sales teams focus on conversions, PR on media coverage, digital on engagement metrics. Each department has its own priorities, vocabulary, and success measures. The IMC manager's first challenge is creating shared goals that all teams can rally behind, then establishing processes that encourage collaboration rather than competition.

Regular cross-functional meetings form the backbone of integration. These aren't status updates where departments take turns reporting, but working sessions focused on solving challenges together. A creative team might explain why certain visual concepts test well, while analytics shares which messages drive conversions, and PR identifies media hooks that could amplify both. This knowledge sharing sparks ideas no single team would develop alone.

Collaboration tools create virtual bridges between departments. Cloud-based platforms allow real-time feedback on assets, shared calendars surface timing opportunities, and internal social networks help teams understand each other's work. When the email marketer sees the PR team landing major coverage, they can quickly adapt their content to leverage it - something that rarely happens when teams work in isolation.

Conflict resolution becomes an essential skill. With multiple perspectives come inevitable disagreements about priorities or approaches. Effective IMC managers facilitate solutions that serve the overall campaign rather than letting powerful departments dominate. This might mean mediating between a brand team wanting polished messaging and a social team advocating for raw authenticity, finding the sweet spot that satisfies both objectives.

Managing External Agencies: Creating Unified Partners

Most brands work with multiple specialized agencies - creative, media buying, PR, digital, and more. Left to themselves, these agencies will optimize for their particular slice of the campaign, often at the expense of integration. The IMC manager must transform them from vendors into true partners working toward shared goals.

The agency briefing process sets the tone for integration. Rather than briefing each agency separately, bring them together for a unified kickoff where they hear the same objectives, see the same customer insights, and understand how their work fits into the whole. This shared foundation prevents the all-too-common scenario where agency work feels disjointed despite individual excellence.

Establishing clear roles and touchpoints prevents overlap and gaps. Who leads concept development? How and when do agencies review each other's work? What's the escalation path for conflicts? Documenting these processes upfront saves countless hours of confusion later. Regular cross-agency syncs maintain alignment as campaigns evolve.

Performance incentives should reward integration, not just individual results. If the media agency gets bonuses for low-cost impressions regardless of how they work with creative, or the PR firm for media hits without considering lead quality, their priorities won't align. Joint KPIs and shared bonuses encourage true collaboration.

The IMC Manager's Multifaceted Role

The IMC manager operates as strategist, diplomat, translator, and air traffic controller all at once. One moment they're explaining customer journey analytics to executives, the next they're helping creative teams understand media buying constraints, then troubleshooting a scheduling conflict between PR and social. This role requires rare versatility across marketing disciplines.

Strategic thinking remains paramount. While managing details, the IMC manager must keep sight of how all pieces contribute to overarching business goals. They continuously ask: Are we reaching the right audiences with the right messages at the right times? Are channels amplifying each other? Are we learning what works to improve future efforts?

Communication skills make or break integration success. The ability to translate between departments - explaining analytics to creatives, creative concepts to data teams, and business impact to executives - ensures everyone stays aligned. Clear, consistent messaging to all stakeholders prevents fragmentation.

Project management provides the operational backbone. Detailed timelines, responsibility matrices, and progress tracking keep complex campaigns on course. The best IMC managers anticipate dependencies - like knowing PR announcements need to precede influencer outreach by two weeks - and build buffers for inevitable delays.

Data synthesis turns information into insight. With inputs flowing in from all channels, the IMC manager identifies patterns and opportunities others miss. Maybe social sentiment analysis reveals unexpected customer concerns that should inform ad messaging, or website behavior suggests email content needs adjustment. Connecting these dots drives continuous optimization.

Leadership inspires teams to collaborate. In organizations accustomed to silos, integration requires cultural change. The IMC manager celebrates cross-team wins, highlights collaboration success stories, and gently but persistently reinforces that "our way" now means "the integrated way."

Practical Integration Tactics

Several proven methods facilitate smooth collaboration. Centralized asset management systems ensure all teams work from approved materials. Shared dashboards provide unified performance views. Cross-training helps teams understand each other's challenges and constraints. Co-location or regular in-person gatherings build relationships that virtual communication can't replace.

Integration checklists prevent oversights. Before any campaign component launches, the checklist confirms alignment with other elements: Do visuals match across channels? Are messages consistent but appropriately adapted? Have all teams reviewed timing? This simple discipline catches most integration failures before they reach audiences.

The most effective IMC managers develop "T-shaped" knowledge - deep expertise in one or two areas (the vertical bar of the T) plus broad understanding across all marketing disciplines (the horizontal top). This enables them to speak each team's language while seeing how everything connects.

Measuring Integration Success

Beyond standard campaign metrics, integration requires specific measures. Cross-channel attribution shows how touchpoints work together. Team surveys assess collaboration health. Asset reuse rates indicate how well content serves multiple purposes. These metrics help prove integration's value and identify areas needing improvement.

The Human Element

Ultimately, integrated marketing succeeds through relationships more than processes. When teams know and trust each other, they share ideas freely, cover for each other's challenges, and celebrate collective wins. The IMC manager's most important job may be fostering this collaborative spirit - the secret sauce that makes all the tools and techniques actually work together.

By mastering these team and agency coordination skills, you'll transform your marketing from a collection of disjointed tactics into a symphony of synchronized efforts that deliver greater impact than the sum of their parts. The following hands-on exercise will let you apply these principles to create your own integrated campaign plan, experiencing both the challenges and rewards of true marketing integration.

Hands-On Exercise: Integrated Campaign Planning Blueprint

Scenario: You're launching "EcoCharge" - a new line of sustainable phone accessories (cases, chargers, screen protectors) made from recycled materials. The campaign must drive both immediate sales and long-term brand awareness for this new product line.

Step 1: Campaign Foundation

- **Objective:** Achieve $500K in sales within 3 months while establishing EcoCharge as the most trusted sustainable tech accessory brand among eco-conscious millennials

- **Core Message:** "Protect your phone while protecting the planet - premium performance without the environmental guilt"

- **Key Channels:** Social media (Instagram/TikTok), influencer partnerships, eco-focused blogs, retail POP displays, Amazon storefront

Step 2: Timeline Development

Month 1 - Awareness Building

- Week 1-2:

- PR: Seed products to 20 micro-influencers (5K-50K followers) in sustainability space

- Social: Launch "Trash to Treasure" behind-the-scenes content showing manufacturing process

- o Email: Send educational content to existing customers about e-waste problem

- Week 3-4:

- o Advertising: Initiate Instagram/TikTok awareness ads with "Did You Know?" facts about tech waste

- o Retail: Place counter displays in 50 partner stores with QR codes to digital content

- o PR: Secure 3 features in eco-conscious digital magazines

Month 2 - Consideration & Conversion

- Week 5-6:

- o Social: Launch UGC contest "Show Your EcoStyle" with product giveaways

- o Email: Send comparison guide vs. conventional accessories

- o Advertising: Retarget website visitors with demo videos

- Week 7-8:

- o Influencers: 3 macro-influencers (100K+ followers) post authentic reviews

- o Sales: Limited-time bundle pricing on case+charger combos

- o PR: Place op-ed by CEO on sustainable tech trends

Month 3 - Retention & Advocacy

- Week 9-10:

- Email: Send recycling program details to purchasers

- Social: Share customer testimonials and repurpose UGC

- Advertising: Remarket to past purchasers with accessory care tips

- Week 11-12:

- PR: Announce "1,000 pounds of ocean plastic collected" milestone

- Social: Launch loyalty program for returning customers

- Content: Publish "Year One Impact Report" infographic

Step 3: Budget Allocation ($150K Total)

Paid Media - 40% ($60K)

- Social advertising: $35K (60% Instagram, 40% TikTok)

- Search/display ads: $15K

- Influencer fees: $10K (for macro-influencers)

Owned/Earned - 35% ($52.5K)

- Content production: $20K (photography, videos, graphics)

- PR agency: $15K

- Email/SMS platform: $7.5K

- UGC incentives: $10K (giveaways, rewards)

Retail/Experiential - 15% ($22.5K)

- POP displays: $12K

- In-store demos: $7.5K

- Packaging design: $3K

Measurement/Optimization - 10% ($15K)

- Analytics tools: $5K

- A/B testing: $7K

- Survey research: $3K

Integration Checklist:

- All creative uses consistent color palette (earth tones + electric green accent)

- Unified hashtag #ChargeWithPurpose across channels

- QR codes on physical materials link to specific landing pages

- Weekly cross-team syncs to share insights and adjust

- Centralized content hub for all assets

Performance Tracking:

- Primary KPI: Revenue from EcoCharge line

- Secondary: Social engagement rate, UGC submissions

- Tertiary: Earned media value, retail partner feedback

Pro Tip: Build in 15% budget flexibility to double down on top-performing channels after Month 1 results.

Module 4: Performance Measurement and Continuous Improvement

Lesson 1: Analytics and Tracking Tools

Lesson 2: Smart Reporting

Lesson 3: Optimization and Strategy Adjustment

Evaluation Task

Module 4: Performance Measurement and Continuous Improvement

Imagine you're a chef preparing an elaborate meal for important guests. You wouldn't just serve the food and walk away - you'd watch which dishes get devoured, notice which flavors get complimented, and observe which plates come back half-eaten. This final module is about developing that same intuitive sense for your marketing campaigns - learning to read the signals, interpret what they mean, and continuously refine your approach based on real-world feedback.

In today's digital landscape, every marketing interaction leaves breadcrumbs of data behind. The difference between good and great marketers isn't who has access to this information (everyone does), but who knows how to connect these dots into meaningful insights that drive smarter decisions. This module will transform you from someone who simply collects metrics to a strategic interpreter who can diagnose what's working, pinpoint what's not, and prescribe precise improvements.

We'll start by exploring the marketing intelligence toolkit - from familiar platforms like Google Analytics to specialized PR monitoring tools that track earned media value. But we'll go far beyond button-clicking tutorials to focus on how these tools work together to give you a complete picture of cross-channel performance. You'll learn how to set up tracking that reveals how your Instagram ads influence website behavior, how your PR coverage impacts search traffic, and how your email campaigns affect retail sales.

Then we'll shift to making sense of all this data through smart reporting. This isn't about creating pretty dashboards (though visualization matters), but about crafting compelling narratives that connect marketing activities to business outcomes. You'll discover how to highlight the insights that matter most to different stakeholders - why the CEO cares about different metrics than your creative team, and how to speak to each audience effectively.

The real magic happens in our optimization lessons, where we move from observation to action. Through real campaign examples, you'll see how A/B testing can settle internal debates about messaging, how incremental refinements compound into major results over time, and when it makes sense to pivot entirely versus stay the course. The best marketers aren't those with perfect first attempts, but those who learn fastest from what the data tells them.

Your final evaluation task will challenge you to play campaign doctor - examining real marketing efforts to diagnose weaknesses and prescribe data-backed improvements. This practical application ensures you don't just understand these concepts theoretically, but develop the critical eye needed to continuously elevate your marketing effectiveness.

As we begin this measurement journey, remember: data without insight is noise, and insight without action is wasted potential. By the end of this module, you'll be equipped to close that loop - turning campaign post-mortems into launchpads for your next marketing breakthrough. Let's dive in.

Lesson 1: Analytics and Tracking Tools for IMC Success

The modern marketer's toolkit resembles a high-tech control center more than the simple spreadsheets of years past. Today's analytics and tracking tools provide unprecedented visibility into how audiences interact with your brand across every touchpoint. But with great power comes great responsibility - the responsibility to choose the right tools, implement them properly, and interpret their signals accurately to guide your integrated marketing strategy.

Google Analytics: The Digital Marketing Compass

Google Analytics serves as the foundational tool for understanding customer journeys across digital properties. Beyond basic traffic counts, its true power lies in revealing how different marketing channels work together to drive conversions. The multi-channel funnel reports show you that a customer might first discover your brand through organic search, return via a social media ad, then finally convert after receiving an email. This insight helps you properly value each touchpoint rather than just crediting the final interaction.

Setting up goals and conversions transforms raw data into actionable business intelligence. Whether tracking newsletter signups, content downloads, or purchases, these defined success metrics allow you to calculate ROI for different campaigns. Enhanced ecommerce tracking takes this further by revealing which products sell best to which audience segments at what times - intelligence that should inform both your marketing and product development.

Custom dashboards save marketers from drowning in data overload. Rather than sifting through hundreds of reports, you can create tailored views showing exactly the metrics that matter for your specific campaigns. An ecommerce manager might prioritize conversion rates and average order value, while a content marketer focuses on engagement time and scroll depth. These focused views help different team members stay aligned on shared objectives while monitoring what matters most for their specific roles.

The audience reports provide a goldmine of customer intelligence. You can analyze behavior by geography, device, acquisition channel, and countless other dimensions. Discovering that mobile users from social media have 30% higher conversion rates than those from email, for example, should immediately inform your channel allocation decisions. This data helps you continually refine your understanding of who your best customers are and how they prefer to engage.

PR Monitoring Tools: Measuring the Immeasurable

While digital channels provide clean metrics, public relations has traditionally been harder to quantify. Modern PR monitoring tools solve this by tracking media impressions, sentiment analysis, and share of voice across online publications, social media, and broadcast outlets. These tools scan millions of sources to find where and how your brand is being mentioned, then analyze whether the coverage is positive, neutral, or negative.

Sentiment analysis algorithms have grown sophisticated enough to detect subtle tone differences that indicate whether coverage is truly favorable. A news article might mention your brand frequently but with skeptical language, while another with fewer mentions might carry enthusiastic endorsements. Understanding this distinction prevents you from overvaluing sheer volume of coverage.

Share of voice metrics compare your media presence to competitors in your industry. If you're launching a new product line, you'll want to track whether your share of category conversations increases relative to established players. These tools can also identify influential journalists and bloggers who drive disproportionate attention in your space - valuable targets for future outreach.

Advanced PR platforms now integrate with web analytics to connect media coverage to concrete business outcomes. You can track spikes in website traffic following major placements, or see if certain publications drive higher-quality leads than others. This helps justify PR investments by showing their impact beyond vague "awareness" benefits.

Ad Management Platforms: Beyond Basic Metrics

Today's ad platforms offer far more than just click-through rates and impression counts. The latest campaign managers provide cross-channel attribution, creative performance insights, and predictive budgeting tools that automate optimization. Facebook's Ads Manager, for example, can show you not just how many leads your campaign generated, but what those leads did afterward - how many made purchases, at what average value, and over what timeframe.

Programmatic buying platforms take this further by using machine learning to automatically adjust bids across thousands of audience segments in real time. These systems can detect that professionals aged 30-45 in urban areas respond best to your sustainability message, then allocate more budget to those high-potential groups while pulling back on poorer performers. The marketer's role shifts from manual tweaking to setting the right strategic parameters and creative direction.

Creative analytics represent an often-overlooked goldmine. Many platforms now provide heatmaps showing which parts of your ads get the most attention, how long viewers watch your videos before dropping off, and which visual elements correlate with conversions. This takes the guesswork out of creative optimization - you'll know definitively whether product shots or lifestyle images work better, whether short or long copy performs better, and which calls-to-action resonate most.

The Power of Integration

The real magic happens when these tools work together through proper integration. Connecting your ad platforms to Google Analytics via UTM parameters lets you see the full customer journey from first impression to final purchase. Linking your PR monitoring to your CRM reveals how media coverage influences lead quality. Unified dashboards that pull data from all sources help you spot trends and correlations that would remain invisible when looking at channels separately.

Tag management systems like Google Tag Manager simplify this integration by letting you deploy tracking codes across all your digital properties without constant developer involvement. You can quickly add event tracking for a new campaign landing page, set up scroll depth measurement for important content, or create custom conversions - all through a user-friendly interface.

Choosing the Right Stack

With countless tools available, selection requires careful consideration of your specific needs. Enterprise-level suites like Adobe Analytics offer powerful customization but require significant implementation resources. Mid-market options like HubSpot provide good balance of capability and usability for growing businesses. Small businesses might start with Google's free tools before graduating to more advanced platforms.

The key is ensuring your tools can talk to each other through APIs or integration platforms. A disconnected toolset creates data silos that undermine integrated marketing. Regular audits of your tech stack help identify redundant tools, missing capabilities, and integration opportunities that could provide more complete visibility.

Implementation Best Practices

Even the best tools fail when implemented poorly. Consistent naming conventions for campaigns and channels prevent reporting confusion. Proper conversion tracking ensures you're measuring what truly matters. Regular data quality checks catch tracking errors before they distort decisions. And documented processes ensure continuity when team members change.

Privacy compliance has become non-negotiable. With GDPR, CCPA and other regulations, you must ensure your tracking respects user consent preferences. Cookie management solutions help balance measurement needs with compliance requirements, while still providing actionable insights.

From Data to Decisions

The ultimate test of any analytics tool is whether it leads to better marketing decisions. Great marketers don't just collect data - they interrogate it. Why did bounce rates increase last week? Which content types drive the most qualified leads? How does mobile behavior differ from desktop? Constant questioning turns raw numbers into strategic insights that fuel continuous improvement in your integrated campaigns.

By mastering these tools and asking the right questions, you'll transform from a marketer who hopes campaigns work to one who knows why they work - and how to make them work even better. This foundation of measurement literacy prepares you for the next step: turning these insights into compelling reports that drive organizational alignment and action.

Lesson 2: Smart Reporting - Transforming Data into Strategic Insights

Data means nothing without context. Smart reporting bridges the gap between raw numbers and actionable marketing intelligence. This process goes far beyond simply compiling statistics into slides—it's about crafting a clear narrative that reveals what's truly working in your integrated campaigns, what needs adjustment, and why. The best reports don't just inform— they inspire action and alignment across your entire organization.

The Foundation of Impactful Reporting

Start by understanding your audience. The C-suite needs different insights than your creative team. Executives want to see how marketing contributes to revenue growth and market share. Channel managers need granular performance details to optimize tactics. Smart reporting tailors the presentation of data to each stakeholder's priorities while maintaining a consistent truth about campaign performance.

Structure reports around business objectives, not just activities. Instead of leading with "We sent 5 emails this month," focus on "Email campaigns contributed to 28% of quarterly revenue, with the nurturing series outperforming promotional blasts by 3:1." This keeps everyone focused on outcomes rather than outputs. Use the inverted pyramid approach—lead with high-impact findings, then provide supporting details for those who need to dive deeper.

Identifying What Works

Look beyond surface-level metrics to find true drivers of success. A social media post with high engagement might seem successful, but does it actually move people toward conversion? A PR placement with wide reach might impress, but did it reach your target audience? Smart reporting connects channel metrics to business outcomes through:

- **Conversion Path Analysis:** Mapping how different touchpoints work together to guide customers

- **Content Performance:** Identifying which messages and formats resonate best with each segment

- **Channel Synergies:** Revealing how combinations of tactics outperform single channels

Use benchmarks to contextualize results. Is your 2% email click-through rate good? That depends — if your industry averages 1.5%, it's strong; if competitors achieve 3.5%, there's room for improvement. Internal benchmarks matter too — tracking performance trends over time shows whether you're improving.

Spotting What Doesn't Work

The most valuable insights often come from understanding failures. Smart reporting surfaces underperforming elements without assigning blame, focusing instead on learning opportunities. Look for:

- **Unexpected Drops:** Sudden changes in performance often indicate technical issues or market shifts

- **Consistent Underperformers:** Tactics that repeatedly miss targets may need reinvention

- **Opportunity Gaps:** Areas where competitors outperform you reveal potential growth areas

Present challenges with solutions. Instead of just reporting "Facebook ads underperformed," add "Creative fatigue appears after 3 weeks—recommend refreshing visuals monthly and testing new audience segments." This maintains a constructive, forward-looking tone.

Visual Storytelling Techniques

The human brain processes visuals 60,000 times faster than text. Effective reports use:

- **Comparison Charts:** Show performance before/after changes

- **Flow Diagrams:** Illustrate customer journeys across touchpoints

- **Heat Maps:** Reveal patterns in engagement or geographic response

- **Progress Dials:** Demonstrate goal achievement at a glance

Keep visuals clean and focused. Avoid chart junk—extra elements that don't convey information. Use consistent color coding (green for positive, red for negative) across all reports to speed interpretation.

Automation with Human Insight

While dashboards provide real-time monitoring, smart reporting adds human analysis to answer "why" behind the numbers. Schedule:

- **Weekly Snapshots:** Quick performance pulse checks

- **Monthly Deep Dives:** Comprehensive analysis with recommendations

- **Quarterly Reviews:** Strategic pattern identification and planning

Build commentary that highlights connections between activities and results. "The 22% sales increase in March correlated with our influencer campaign and subsequent retargeting efforts, particularly among 25-34 year-olds in urban areas."

Creating Actionable Recommendations

The best reports conclude with clear next steps prioritized by potential impact:

1. **Continue:** What's working well that we should expand?

2. **Adjust:** What needs optimization?

3. **Stop:** What's not delivering and should be discontinued?

4. **Test:** What new opportunities should we explore?

This structure turns insights into an execution roadmap that keeps your integrated marketing continuously improving.

Evaluation Task Preview:

In the upcoming exercise, you'll analyze real campaign data to identify three strengths to build upon and three areas for improvement, developing specific recommendations for each. This practical application will sharpen your ability to extract meaningful insights from marketing performance data.

Remember — smart reporting isn't about proving you were right. It's about discovering what's truly effective so you can do more of it. The most successful marketers aren't those with perfect campaigns, but those who learn fastest from their results.

Lesson 3: Optimization and Strategy Adjustment

The most successful marketing campaigns aren't those that start strong — they're the ones that get smarter as they go. Optimization transforms good campaigns into great ones through continuous refinement based on real-world performance. This process combines the scientific rigor of A/B testing with the creative finesse of message refinement, creating a powerful engine for incremental improvement that compounds into significant results over time.

A/B Testing: The Science of Smarter Decisions

A/B testing cuts through opinions and assumptions by letting your audience tell you what works. The basic premise — showing different versions to similar audiences and measuring which performs better — seems simple, but mastering it requires strategic thinking.

What to Test Across Channels:

- *Email:* Subject lines, sender names, send times, content length, CTA placement

- *Digital Ads:* Visual styles, messaging angles, audience segments, landing pages

- *Social Media:* Post formats, hashtag strategies, video lengths, caption styles

- *Website:* Navigation layouts, form lengths, button colors, content organization

Advanced Testing Approaches

Multivariate testing examines how multiple elements interact — does that bold headline work better with the product image or lifestyle shot? Sequential testing reveals how the same user responds to different messages over time. Bandit algorithms automatically shift traffic to better-performing variants during the test itself.

Interpreting Results Correctly

Statistical significance separates real insights from random noise. A 5% difference with 85% confidence means keep testing; that same difference with 95% confidence means you can act. Consider both practical significance (will this move the needle?) and implementation cost before making changes.

Message Refinement: The Art of Continuous Improvement

Great messaging evolves through careful iteration. Performance data shows what's working at the tactical level, while brand tracking studies monitor higher-level perception shifts.

The Refinement Process

1. *Audit* existing messaging performance across all touchpoints

2. *Identify* underperforming elements and inconsistencies

3. *Hypothesize* improvements based on audience insights

4. *Test* variations in controlled environments

5. *Implement* winners across relevant channels

6. *Monitor* impact and prepare for next refinement cycle

Message Adaptation vs. Consistency

While core value propositions should remain stable, their expression needs regular refreshing to avoid fatigue. A financial services brand might consistently communicate "security" but rotate how it demonstrates this — through customer stories one quarter, expert endorsements the next, then innovative features after that.

Optimizing Across the Customer Journey

Different messages work at different stages:

- *Awareness:* Focus on emotional hooks and audience needs

- *Consideration:* Emphasize differentiation and proof points

- *Decision:* Highlight risk reduction and immediate value

- *Retention:* Reinforce community and ongoing benefits

Bringing It All Together

The companies that excel at integrated marketing treat every campaign as a learning opportunity. They establish feedback loops where:

1. Performance data informs optimization tests

2. Test results guide message refinements

3. Refined messages generate new performance data

This creates a virtuous cycle of continuous improvement where each iteration builds on the last. The key is maintaining detailed documentation of what's been tried and what's been learned — building institutional knowledge that prevents repeating past mistakes while replicating past successes.

Evaluation Task Preview:

Your upcoming analysis will challenge you to examine real campaign data, identify optimization opportunities, and propose specific A/B tests to improve results. This practical application will develop your ability to turn insights into action — the hallmark of truly data-driven marketing.

Remember — perfection isn't the goal. Progress is. Small, consistent improvements compound into massive advantages over time. The marketers who thrive aren't those who create flawless first drafts, but those who develop the discipline and systems to keep making their work better and better.

Evaluation Task: Campaign Performance Analysis & Optimization Plan

Step 1: Select a Real Campaign for Analysis
Choose either:
a) A recent integrated campaign from your organization
b) A publicly documented campaign from a major brand
c) The EcoCharge campaign from our earlier exercise

Part A: Performance Assessment (40 points)

1. **Campaign Background** (5 points)

o Brand name & product/service

o Primary objectives (awareness, leads, sales, etc.)

o Duration and channels used

2. **Data Collection** (10 points)

o Identify 3 key metrics tracked for each channel

o Note any missing data points that would have been valuable

3. **Success Evaluation** (15 points)

o Which elements exceeded expectations? Why?

o Which underperformed? Potential reasons?

o How did channels work together (or fail to)?

4. **Competitive Context** (10 points)

- How did this perform vs. industry benchmarks?

- Did competitors run similar campaigns? Compare results

Part B: Improvement Opportunities (60 points)

1. **Technical Optimization** (15 points)

- Identify 3 tracking/measurement gaps to fix

- Propose specific tools or processes to address them

2. **Creative/Messaging Adjustments** (20 points)

- Based on performance data, suggest:

  - 2 underperforming messages to revise

  - 1 new message variation to test

  - 1 visual element to improve

3. **Channel Optimization** (15 points)

- Recommend:

  - 1 channel to increase investment in (with justification)

  - 1 channel to reduce or eliminate

  - 1 new channel to test

4. **Testing Plan** (10 points)

- Design 2 specific A/B tests to run in next iteration

- For each, specify:

- What you're testing (subject line? image? audience?)

- How you'll measure success

- Minimum sample size/duration

Submission Format:

- 3-5 page report OR

- 10-12 slide presentation OR

- Video analysis (8-10 minutes)

Grading Rubric:
✓ Depth of analysis (30%)
✓ Data-driven recommendations (30%)
✓ Feasibility of improvements (20%)
✓ Clarity of presentation (20%)

Pro Tip: Use the "Stop-Start-Continue" framework:

- **Stop** 3 things that didn't work

- **Start** 3 new optimizations

- **Continue** 3 successful elements

This evaluation will test your ability to move from raw data to strategic insights to actionable plans — the complete performance improvement cycle covered in this module.

Capstone Project

Design an Integrated Marketing Communications campaign for a new or existing business. Your project should include:

- Advertising elements

- Public Relations strategies

- Digital channel integration

- Timeline and budget

- Consistent messaging across all platforms

About the author

Dr. Aziza Tawfiq Abdelghafar, a PhD holder from Ain Shams University, is an expert in strategic planning, marketing, and administrative sciences. With extensive experience in academia, industry, and entrepreneurship, she has authored specialized books and research papers. A sought-after speaker, she has contributed to scientific and industrial conferences, shaping the future of marketing and management sciences.

www.ingramcontent.com/pod-product-compliance
Lightning Source LLC
Chambersburg PA
CBHW071002050326
40689CB00014B/3457